hamly  coolers,
d soups

100 HEALTH-BOOSTING DRINKS

An Hachette UK company
www.hachette.co.uk

First published in Great Britain in 2005 by
Hamlyn, a division of Octopus Publishing Group Ltd
Endeavour House
189 Shaftesbury Avenue
London WC2H 8JY
www.octopusbooks.co.uk

This edition published in 2015

ISBN 978-0-60063-004-3

A CIP catalogue record for this book is available from
the British Library

Printed and bound in China

10 9 8 7 6 5 4 3 2 1

All reasonable care has been taken in the preparation
of this book but the information it contains is not
intended to take the place of treatment by a qualified
medical practitioner.

Contents

4 introduction

12 boost your immunity

48 enhance your energy

80 first aid

116 bright start

154 body, spirit and soul soothers

190 detox solutions

222 index

224 acknowledgements

introduction

We know we should eat five portions of fruit and vegetables a day, but few of us do. *100 Health-boosting drinks* will show you how to get the fruit and vegetables you need in a delicious and nutritious form.

What are health-boosting drinks?

They are juices, smoothies, coolers, infusions and soups made from nutritious ingredients and designed to maintain optimum health.

JUICES are simple to make with a juicer using just about any fruit or vegetable.

SMOOTHIES are juices or whole pieces of fruit blended to make thicker drinks.

COOLERS are long, refreshing drinks often made with sparkling water and usually served over ice.

INFUSIONS are made with boiling water. The nutrients can be easily absorbed when drunk.

SOUPS offer a comforting way to eat plenty of ingredients with health-giving properties.

How do they benefit health?

The main benefits of health-boosting drinks are the vitamins, minerals and enzymes contained in the fruits and vegetables. As the produce is generally in a raw state, nearly all of the nutrients are retained.

- **PROTECTION AGAINST DISEASE** A diet rich in fruit and vegetables can prevent and help to cure a range of ailments. Phytochemicals from plants hold the key to preventing some of our most deadly diseases such as heart disease and cancer as well as other ailments and allergies.
- **IMMUNITY BOOSTING** Vegetables and fruit are sources of nutrients, such as vitamins C and E, betacarotene and minerals. These help to keep you in tiptop health and boost your immunity so you don't succumb to every virus around.
- **ENERGY ENHANCING** These drinks keep you feeling full longer than 'empty' snacks like crisps and chocolate. The nutrients in them give you an energy boost and if you consume them regularly, you will have more energy to face each day.
- **EXTRA FLUIDS** Water is vital for health. It makes up more than 65 per cent of our cells, and as much as 80 per cent of some brain cells. These drinks contain plenty of fluids and don't have the dehydrating effects of tea, coffee and fizzy drinks.
- **ANTI-AGEING BENEFITS** The antioxidants in fruit and vegetables are nature's secret weapons against ageing and have been found to protect against wrinkles, sagging skin, loss of muscle tone, age spots and the onset of many age-related diseases.

- **DETOX** Many of the drinks in this book have a detox effect, helping to clear toxins in the body, leaving you refreshed and rejuvenated.
- **WEIGHT LOSS** Health-boosting drinks are great in a weight-loss programme as they are satisfying and nutritious. However, be sure to include a balance of foods to maintain healthy cells.

Choosing ingredients

Choose the freshest ingredients as nutrients disappear after fruit and vegetables are picked. Frozen fruit and vegetables are a good second choice if they have been frozen immediately after picking. They often contain more vitamins and minerals than fresh produce that is past its best.

Buying organic

Many people prefer to buy organic and research has shown that levels of zinc, vitamin C and carotene are higher in organic produce. Another advantage is that many non-organic fruits and vegetables contain pesticides, and do not need to be peeled before being eaten. As most enzymes, vitamins and minerals lie just below the surface of the skin, peeling is counter-productive. It is much better to buy organic. Scrub all fruit and vegetables under warm running water.

Making juices

You will need an electric juicer to separate the juice from the pulp. There are two basic types: centrifugal juicers and masticating juicers. Centrifugal juicers are widely available and affordable while masticating juicers extract a little more juice but are more expensive. Choose a model that is easy to clean and that takes relatively large pieces of fruit and vegetable to reduce the amount of chopping, and the time it takes to feed the produce through the machine.

Cut foods into manageable pieces including the skin and pips if the produce is organic or has been thoroughly scrubbed. Don't include the skin of pineapple, mango, papaya, orange, lemon or banana and remove stones from apricots, peaches, mangoes, avocados and plums.

5

key ingredients

ingredient	nutrients	benefits
Almonds	Calcium, magnesium, phosphorus, zinc, potassium, folic acid, vitamins B12, B3, E	Reduce risk of heart disease, lower cholesterol, anticancer
Apple	Calcium, vitamin C, magnesium, betacarotene, pectin	Cleansing, high fibre, antioxidant, anti-inflammatory, lowers cholesterol, anticancer, counters diarrhoea and constipation, helps joint problems, prevents disease
Apricot	Betacarotene, iron, potassium, folic acid, boron, copper, calcium, vitamin C	Regulates blood pressure, soluble fibre, antioxidant
Asparagus	Potassium, folic acid, betacarotene, vitamins C, K	Mild laxative, stimulates the kidneys, antibacterial
Avocado	Vitamins E, C, B6, potassium, folic acid, iron	Reduces cholesterol and atherosclerosis, antioxidant, easy on digestion, balances acid-alkaline content
Banana	Potassium, vitamins B6, C, tryptophan, betacarotene	Maintains bowel health, boosts blood sugar levels, promotes sleep, lowers cholesterol, natural antibiotic
Barley	Calcium, iron, magnesium, zinc, folic acid, potassium, phosphorus, B vitamins	Lowers oestrogen levels, soluble fibre, may help to avoid heart disease, heals stomach ulcers
Beetroot	Calcium, magnesium, iron, potassium, folic acid, vitamin C	Cleansing, fortifies blood, eliminates kidney stones, detoxifies the liver
Black pepper	Calcium, magnesium, potassium, manganese, phosphorus	Digestive stimulant, antioxidant, antibacterial
Blackberries	Betacarotene, vitamins C and E, calcium, magnesium, phosphorus, potassium, sodium	Antioxidant, boost immune system, anti-ageing
Blueberries	Vitamin C, betacarotene	Antioxidant, anti-inflammatory, anticoagulant, combats diarrhoea, antibacterial, anti-ageing
Broccoli	Folic acid, betacarotene, magnesium, calcium, vitamins C, B3, B5, phosphorus	Anticancer, antioxidant, antibiotic, antiviral, cleanses liver and intestines
Cabbage	Calcium, magnesium, vitamins C, E, K, folic acid, potassium, betacarotene	Detoxifies colon, antiviral, supports immune system, antioxidant, antibacterial, relieves gastric ulcers

Carrot	Betacarotene, calcium, potassium, magnesium	Detoxifier, supports liver and digestive tract, antibacterial, antiviral
Celery	Folic acid, vitamin B3, sodium, potassium	Anticancer, lowers blood pressure, diuretic, anti-inflammatory
Cinnamon	Calcium, iron, potassium	Stimulates digestive system, relieves nausea
Coconut	Magnesium, potassium, phosphorus, zinc, folic acid, vitamin C	Regulates thyroid function
Coriander	Vitamin C, potassium	Good for circulatory system, digestive system and the skin, relieves migraines
Cranberries	Potassium, betacarotene, vitamin C	Reduce bladder infections, help to maintain a healthy heart, anti-inflammatory, antiviral, antibacterial
Cucumber	Potassium, betacarotene	Diuretic, lowers blood pressure, benefits kidneys
Fennel	Folic acid, sodium, vitamin C, calcium, magnesium, potassium	Antispasmodic, rebalances hormones in menopausal women, helps break down fat
Garlic	Calcium, potassium, vitamin C, allicin	Antibacterial, antiviral, antiseptic, lowers cholesterol, thins blood, supports immune system
Ginger	Calcium, magnesium, potassium	Antispasmodic, alleviates nausea and menstrual cramps, relieves indigestion and flatulence, discourages blood clots, stimulates circulation
Grapefruit	Calcium, magnesium, potassium, vitamin C	May reduce the risk of some cancers, helps arthritis, improves blood circulation, lowers cholesterol levels
Grapes	Glucose, fructose, potassium, vitamin C, carotene	Fights carcinogens, relieves arthritis, lowers blood pressure and helps urinary disorders
Horseradish	Vitamin C, potassium	Improves circulation, regulates blood pressure, relieves symptoms of flu. Lowers cholesterol, anticancer
Lemons/limes	Potassium, vitamin C	Lower cholesterol, anticancer
Lentils	Iron, potassium, folate, zinc, B vitamins	Control blood sugar, lower cholestrol, aid bowel health
Mango	Vitamin C, betacarotene	Supports kidneys, aids digestion, good blood cleanser
Melon	Calcium, potassium, vitamin C, betacarotene	Anticoagulant, lowers heart disease risk, cleanses and rehydrates
Mushrooms	Zinc, calcium, iron, magnesium, folic acid, B vitamins	Lower cholesterol, support immune function
Onions	Quercetin, folic acid, potassium, calcium, betacarotene, magnesium	Reduce risk of heart disease, anticancer, relieve congestion in airways

Oranges	Vitamin C, betacarotene, folic acid, calcium, potassium	Reduce risk of some cancers, improve circulation, lower cholesterol, stimulate, cleanse, internal antiseptic
Papaya	Vitamin C, betacarotene, calcium, potassium	Aids digestion, soothes internal inflammation, antiparasitic, anticancer, a great detoxifier
Parsley	Folate, vitamin C, iron, calcium	Antioxidant, strengthens, thins and cleanses blood, diuretic, helps kidney function and eases gout
Parsnips	Folate, potassium, vitamins C, E	Fibre, help maintain blood pressure, strengthen blood
Peaches	Carotenes, flavonoids and vitamin C	Good for irritated stomachs and persistent coughs, lower blood pressure, protect against heart disease, anticancer
Pears	Potassium, betacarotene, vitamin C	Steady release of sugar maintains blood sugar levels
Peppers	Potassium, betacarotene, folic acid, vitamin C	Antibacterial, regulate blood pressure, good for circulation, stimulate gastric juices and peristalsis
Pineapple	Vitamin C, bromelain, potassium, betacarotene	Anticoagulant, aids digestion
Raspberries	Ellagic acid, magnesium, potassium, vitamin C	Regulate menstrual cycle, antiviral, help weight loss
Soya milk (plain, unfortified)	Protein, iron, calcium, vitamins D, B12	Reduces risk of heart disease and cancer, lowers cholesterol, helps some menopausal symptoms
Spinach	Potassium, folate, iron, vitamins B, C, betacarotene	Anticancer, strengthens blood, may protect against eye degeneration and heart disease
Strawberries	Vitamins C, A, K, betacarotene, folic acid, potassium	Antioxidant, anticancer, antiviral, antibacterial
Sweet potato	Betacarotene, vitamins C, E, folic acid, calcium, magnesium, potassium	Aids heart health, antioxidants, helps regulate high blood pressure, anti-inflammatory, strengthens blood
Tofu	Iron, protein, potassium, magnesium, calcium, vitamins A, K	Lowers risk of some cancers, helps prevent osteoporosis, controls diabetes and symptoms of the menopause
Tomatoes	Calcium, magnesium, phosphorus, betacarotene, folic acid, vitamin C	May reduce risk of prostate and breast cancer, antiseptic, anti-inflammatory
Wheat	Calcium, iron, magnesium, potassium, phosphorus, zinc, folic acid, manganese, vitamins B5, B6	Organic, untreated wholewheat with bran and germ left intact stimulates the liver and eliminates toxins
Yogurt	Calcium, vitamin D	Soothes intestinal tract, promotes good bacteria

rda table

vitamin/rda	function	food sources
vitamin A (retinol) 600 mcg	Promotes eye health; antioxidant with immunity-boosting function	Liver, dairy products, eggs, oily fish
beta-carotene (pro-vitamin A) 25 mg	Antioxidant, anticancer. The body can convert beta-carotene into vitamin A	All dark green, orange or red fruit and vegetables, e.g. red pepper, pumpkin and spinach
vitamin B1 (thiamine) 0.8 mg	Needed for energy production and for a healthy nervous system	Milk, meat, wholegrain/fortified breakfast cereal, dried fruit, nuts, pulses, brown rice, peas and beans
vitamin B2 (riboflavin) 1.3 mg	Helps the body get energy from food. Aids healthy eyes, hair and nails	Milk, liver, kidneys, cheese, fortified breakfast cereal
vitamin B5 (pantothenic acid) No official RDA	Anti-stress vitamin, boosting the metabolism and aiding energy release from food	Liver, kidneys, yeast, wheatgerm, fortified breakfast cereal, wholemeal bread, nuts, pulses, fresh vegetables
vitamin B6 (pyridoxine) 1.2 mg	Balances hormonal change in women and helps cell production	Numerous foods, including meat, wholemeal bread, brown rice, bananas and pulses
vitamin B12 (cobaldmin) 1.5 mg	Aids red blood cell production and maintenance of healthy nerves	Liver, kidney, oily fish, meat, eggs, dairy products, fortified breakfast cereals
folic acid 200 mg	Prevention of spinal disabilities in the foetus. Aids red blood cell production and energy release from food	Green leafy vegetables, liver, pulses, eggs, wholemeal cereals, orange juice, wheatgerm
vitamin C (ascorbic acid) 40 mg	Protects against some cancers and coronary heart disease. Helps maintain healthy bones, teeth and gums	Most fruit and vegetables – among the best sources are kiwi fruits, citrus fruits, peppers, blackcurrants and strawberries
vitamin D (calciferol) 10 mg	Promotes a healthy nervous system; formation of healthy bones and teeth	Oily fish, dairy products, eggs
vitamin E (tocopherols) 10 mg	Antioxidant. Protects against heart disease and cancer	Vegetable oils, polyunsaturated margarine, wheatgerm, sunflower seeds, hazelnuts, oily fish, wholegrain cereal, eggs, avocado and spinach
vitamin K 10 mg	Necessary in the formation of blood clots when the body needs it	Broccoli, cabbage, spinach, liver, alfafa, tomatoes and kelp

ailment chart

ailment	recommended recipes
Acid stomach	Digestive Duo, Fiery Indian Broth, Herbal Harmony, Tropicana, Tummy Tonic
Allergies	Caribbean Spice, Eat Your Greens
Anaemia	Beet This, Blood Orange, Chill-out, Pecan Punch, Red Devil, Red Wire, Squeaky Green
Arthritis	Acher Shaker, Bean Good, Brain Booster, Caribbean Spice, Chill-out, Karma Kooler, Twister, Zesty Ginger Beer
Asthma	Classic C & C, Hot Stuff, Lentil Power
Bloating/ water retention	Black Bean Bonanza, Cabbage Soup, Dynamic Detox, Evergreen, Feel-good Fennel, Flush-a-bye-baby, Ginger Zinger, Herbal Harmony, The Great Gazpacho
Bronchitis	Citrus Squeeze, Hot Stuff, The Great Gazpacho
Cellulite	Bumpy Ride, Feel-good Fennel, The Great Gazpacho
Cholesterol reduction	Belly Berry, Black Bean Bonanza, Brain Booster, Chill-out, Lentil Power, Purple Passion, Wild Mushroom Dream
Colds and flu	Berry Nice, C for Comfort, Classic C & C, Frisky Sour, Ginger Zinger, Hot Stuff, Passion Fruit Plus, Sweet Stinger, Orient Express
Constipation	Black Bean Bonanza, Cabbage Soup, Feel-good Fennel, Summer Soup, The Great Gazpacho, Way to Go
Cystitis	Cleansing Cranberry, Flush-a-bye-baby, Smooth and Soothing
Detox	Digestive Duo, Dynamic Detox, Flush-a-bye-baby, Freshen Up, Herbal Harmony, Herbi-four, Juicy Lucy, Lemon Barley Water, Orchard Medley, Red Devil, Spring Clean, Squeaky Green, Strawberry Cleanser, Tropical Trio
Diarrhoea	Belly Berry, Purple Passion, Zesty Ginger Beer
Dieting	Cool and Cleansing, Evergreen, Flush-a-bye-baby, Ginger Spice, Karma Kooler
Eczema	Cabbage Soup, Classic C & C
Eyesight	Berry Mull, Caribbean Spice, Carroty Cooler, Chunky Chowder, Classic C & C, Papaya Flyer, Seeing Red, Twister, Vision Impeccable

Haemorrhoids	Brain Booster, Summer Soup, Way to Go
Hangover	Beet This, Classic C & C, Full Tank, Hot Stuff, Karma Kooler, Morning After, Orient Express, Warm and Spicy, Zesty Ginger Beer
Headaches and migraines	Brain Booster, Evergreen, Fever Fusion, The Great Gazpacho
Heart disease	Brain Booster, Bumpy Ride, Classic C & C
High blood pressure	Fruity Filler, Lounge Lizard, Plum Punch, The Great Gazpacho
Hypoglycaemia	Black Bean Bonanza, Chill-out, Chunky Chowder, Minty Magic
Immune system	Frisky Sour, Ginger Zinger, Golden Fizz, Mango Magic, Morning After, Passion Fruit Plus, Protein Pack, Quick Hit, Sergeant Pepper, Tchae Trio, Time Out, Tomato Tonic, What's Up Broc?
Insomnia	Pillow Talk, Sleeping Beauty, Sleep Tight, Smooth Operator, Soothing Brew
Irritable Bowel Syndrome	Mussel Power, Spring Clean
Lethargy	Power Pack, Juicy Lucy, Vitamin Vitality, Energy Bubble, Red Wire, Tongue Tingler
Low energy	Brain Booster, Energy Fizz, Feel-good Fennel, High Kick, Rose Royce, Time Out, The Great Gazpacho
Low fertility	Green Dream, Mussel Power, Passion Thriller, Tofu and Papaya Soup
Menopause	Brain Booster, Eat Your Greens, Mussel Power
Osteoporosis	Chill-out, Lentil Power, Mango Magic, Minty Magic, Caribbean Spice, Fiery Indian Broth
PMT	Brain Booster, Caribbean Spice, Sleep Tight
Pregnancy care	Squeaky Green
Seasonal Affective Disorder	Berried Treasure, Black Bean Bonanza, Chunky Veggie Chowder, Recovery, Smooth and Soothing, Smooth Operator, Brain Booster
Sinusitis	Ginger Spice, Hot Stuff, Lentil Power
Skin disorders	Beauty Fuel, Carroty Cooler, Green Dream, Herbi-four, Passion Thriller, Peach Dream, Protein Pack, Sour Power
Stress	Evergreen, Feelin' Good, Feel-good Fennel, Hula Kula, Lounge Lizard, Papaya Flyer, Pillow Talk, Smooth Operator, Soothing Brew
Weight gain	Eat Your Greens, Feel-good Fennel, Green Dream, Minty Magic, Orient Express, Passion Thriller, Sweet Chariot

frisky sour

150 g (5 oz) papaya

150 g (5 oz) grapefruit

150 g (5 oz) raspberries

½ lime, plus slices to decorate

ice cubes

A great tonic for colds and flu. If you're run down and haven't been eating a balanced diet, your immune system becomes more susceptible – try this.

1 Scoop out the papaya flesh and juice it with the grapefruit (with the pith left on) and the raspberries.

2 Squeeze in the juice of the lime and mix. Serve with ice cubes and decorate with lime slices.

makes 200 ml (7 fl oz)

NUTRITIONAL CONTENT: **energy** 152 kcals ǀ **calcium** 110 mg ǀ **magnesium** 55 mg ǀ **zinc** 1.1 mg ǀ **vitamin C** 219 mg ǀ **vitamin A** 183 mcg.

sergeant pepper

100 g (3½ oz) red pepper

100 g (3½ oz) yellow pepper

100 g (3½ oz) orange pepper

1 orange

1 tablespoon mint leaves

ice cubes

Another good choice if you're run down and fighting colds and flu. Peppers ward off infection and are natural painkillers.

1 Juice the peppers and orange and serve in a tumbler with ice cubes. Stir in the mint leaves.

makes 200 ml (7 fl oz)

NUTRITIONAL CONTENT: energy 130 kcals I **calcium** 91 mg I **magnesium** 58 mg I **zinc** 0.4 mg I **vitamin C** 466 mg I **vitamin A** 714 mcg.

15

NUTRITIONAL CONTENT: **energy** 99 kcals I **calcium** 86 mg I **magnesium** 39 mg I **zinc** 0.2 mg I **vitamin C** 84 mg I **vitamin A** 108 mcg.

125 g (4 oz) carrot

250 g (8 oz) cantaloupe melon

1 lime, plus wedges to serve

2.5 cm (1 inch) cube of fresh root ginger, roughly chopped

seeds from 1 cardamom pod

ice cubes

A juice rich in antioxidants. The lime encourages the elimination of toxins.

1 Juice the carrot, melon, lime and ginger. Serve in a glass over ice. Decorate with lime wedges and seeds from the cardamom pod.

makes 200 ml (7 fl oz)

ginger zinger

what's up broc?

250 g (8 oz) broccoli

175 g (6 oz) carrot

50 g (2 oz) beetroot

1 coriander sprig, to decorate

Broccoli is a natural antibiotic, and is also powerfully anti-viral, providing an instant boost to your immune system.

1 Juice the broccoli, carrot and beetroot and serve in a tall glass. Decorate with a coriander sprig.

makes 200 ml (7 fl oz)

NUTRITIONAL CONTENT: energy 153 kcals I **calcium** 210 mg I **magnesium** 76 mg I **zinc** 2.1 mg I **vitamin C** 227 mg I **vitamin A** 1796 mcg.

19

time out

100 g (3½ oz) fresh or frozen blackberries

¼ cantaloupe melon, skinned

2 kiwi fruits

Not just a great colour, this juice is loaded with vitamin C, calcium and magnesium, essential for energy production and body cell maintenance.

1 Reserve a few blackberries for decoration, juice the remainder with the melon flesh and kiwi, then put the juices in a blender and process with a couple of ice cubes. Pour into a glass and serve decorated with the reserved blackberries.

makes 250 ml (8 fl oz)

NUTRITIONAL CONTENT: energy 112 kcals | **calcium** 101 mg | **magnesium** 58 mg | **zinc** 0.3 mg | **vitamin C** 125 mg | **vitamin A** 271 mcg.

21

protein pack

150 g (5 oz) frozen mixed summer berries, plus extra, to decorate

300 ml (½ pint) vanilla-flavoured soya milk

1 teaspoon clear honey (optional)

A lovely summer drink rich in zinc and vitamin C, both great for warding off infections. To make it even more nutritious, use a soya milk enriched with calcium.

1 Place the berries, soya milk and honey, if using, in a blender and process until thick. Serve immediately, decorated with berries.

makes 400 ml (14 fl oz)

NUTRITIONAL CONTENT: energy 202 kcals I **calcium** 84 mg I **magnesium** 80 mg I **zinc** 1 mg I **vitamin C** 62 mg I **vitamin A** 8 mcg.

NUTRITIONAL CONTENT: **energy** 218 kcals I **calcium** 74 mg I **magnesium** 68 mg I **zinc** 0.3 mg I **vitamin C** 296 mg I **vitamin A** 461 mcg.

125 g (4 oz) strawberries, hulled

1 small ripe mango, plus extra slices, to decorate

300 ml (½ pint) orange juice

Mango is rich in betacarotene, a precursor of vitamin A. With the vitamin C from the orange juice and strawberries this drink gives a hit of antioxidants, protective against cancers.

1 Roughly chop the strawberries and the mango flesh and freeze for at least 2 hours or overnight.

2 Place them in a blender with the orange juice and process until thick. Decorate with slices of mango.

makes 400 ml (14 fl oz)

quick hit

mango magic

½ large mango

100 ml (3½ fl oz) natural yogurt

100 ml (3½ fl oz) water

1 mint sprig, to decorate

A delicious creamy smoothie loaded with calcium for bones and blood, and rich in protective betacarotene.

1 Blend the mango flesh with the other ingredients until smooth, then serve decorated with a sprig of mint.

makes 350 ml (12 fl oz)

NUTRITIONAL CONTENT: energy 99 kcals I **calcium** 199 mg I **magnesium** 29 mg I **zinc** 0.7 mg I **vitamin C** 29 mg I **vitamin A** 234 mcg.

27

carroty cooler

**250 g (8 oz) cantaloupe melon,
skinned**

**250 ml (8 fl oz) carrot juice,
chilled**

150 ml (¼ pint) orange juice

juice of 2 limes

ice cubes

A refreshing drink stacked with vitamin C and carotenes,
the vitamin A precursors. Vitamin C acts as an internal
antiseptic and is great for warding off infections.

1 Put the melon into a food processor or blender and
process for 1 minute, then add the carrot, orange and
lime juices and process again until thoroughly mixed.
To serve, pour into tall glasses over crushed ice.

makes 600 ml (1 pint)

NUTRITIONAL CONTENT: energy 80 kcals I **calcium** 57 mg I **magnesium** 35 mg I **zinc** 0.2 mg I
vitamin C 87 mg I **vitamin A** 1905 mcg.

29

tomato tonic

150 ml (¼ pint) tomato juice

25 g (1 oz) cucumber, peeled

2 dashes of lemon juice

2 dashes of Worcestershire sauce

salt and pepper

cucumber slice, to decorate

crushed ice

Tasty and refreshing for a hot day, this low-calorie drink supplies vitamin C and a range of other vitamins and minerals.

1 Put a little crushed ice into a blender. Add the tomato juice, cucumber, lemon juice, Worcestershire sauce and salt and pepper to taste and blend well.

2 Pour the drink into a cocktail glass and decorate with a slice of cucumber on the rim.

makes 250 ml (8 fl oz)

NUTRITIONAL CONTENT: energy 30 kcals | calcium 39 mg | magnesium 25 mg | zinc 0.2 mg | vitamin C 16 mg | vitamin A 53 mcg.

31

NUTRITIONAL CONTENT: energy 98 kcals I **calcium** 45 mg I **magnesium** 25 mg I **zinc** 0.5 mg I **vitamin C** 151 mg I **vitamin A** 151 mcg.

1 papaya, peeled, quartered and deseeded

250 ml (8 fl oz) orange juice

sparkling mineral water

sprig of mint, to decorate

ice cubes

A tingly golden cooler stuffed with vitamin C, vitamin A and betacarotenes. It protects against infection and some cancers.

1 Place the papaya and orange juice in a food processor or blender and process for about 30 seconds until smooth.

2 Put 2–3 ice cubes into 2 tall glasses, pour in the drink and top up with sparkling water. Stir and decorate with a mint sprig.

makes 475 ml (16 fl oz)

golden fizz

sweet stinger

1 clementine

4 nettle sprigs

200 ml (7 fl oz) boiling water

mild honey, to sweeten

Gather fresh, young nettle leaves for this mild infusion. You'll need to wear gloves when picking the leaves, but the 'sting' soon goes once the leaves are heated. Like citrus fruits, nettles are rich in vitamin C and minerals, giving your system an invigorating boost.

1 Pare a long strip of rind from the clementine, then halve it and squeeze the juice.

2 Put the clementine rind and nettle sprigs in a cup and pour over the boiling water. Leave to infuse for 3–5 minutes.

3 Lift out the nettle sprigs and stir in the squeezed clementine juice and a little honey to sweeten.

makes 250 ml (8 fl oz)

NUTRITIONAL CONTENT: energy 39 kcals I **calcium** 15 mg I **magnesium** 5 mg I **zinc** 0.1 mg I **vitamin C** 22 mg I **vitamin A** 8 mcg.

35

passion fruit plus

1 lemongrass stalk

200 ml (7 fl oz) boiling water

2 passion fruits

1 lime

2 teaspoons clear honey

This exotic infusion offers a warming way to get plenty of vitamin C. The lemongrass is fresh tasting and aromatic and, like passion fruit, has antiseptic properties.

1 Cut the lemongrass stalk in half lengthways then finely chop one of the halves. Put in a small bowl and pour over the boiling water. Leave to infuse for 3–4 minutes.

2 Halve the passion fruits and scoop the pulp into a tea strainer, set over a cup. Press the pulp with the back of a teaspoon to extract the juice.

3 Add the lime juice to the cup and strain in the lemongrass infusion through the strainer. Add the honey and use the halved lemongrass stalk as a stirrer.

makes 250 ml (8 fl oz)

NUTRITIONAL CONTENT: energy 71 kcals **| calcium** 7 mg **| magnesium** 11 mg **| zinc** 0.5 mg **| vitamin C** 18 mg **| vitamin A** 38 mcg.

37

tchae trio

200 ml (7 fl oz) boiling water

1 green tea bag

2 large parsley sprigs

4 large pineapple sage leaves

2 lemon thyme sprigs

½ teaspoon clear honey

Try a double dose of immune-boosting nutrients with this combination of green tea and healing herbs. Parsley is rich in vitamins A, B and C and has diuretic and cleansing properties. Lemon thyme and pineapple sage are both antiseptic and give this infusion a fresh, tingly aftertaste.

1 Pour the boiling water over the tea bag in a cup and leave to infuse for 1 minute.

2 Lightly crush the parsley and sage leaves between your fingers to bruise them and release the flavour. Add to the cup with the thyme and honey. Leave for 3–4 minutes then drain the teabag and herbs.

makes 200 ml (7 fl oz)

NUTRITIONAL CONTENT: energy 27 kcals | **calcium** 42 mg | **magnesium** 7 mg | **zinc** 0.1 mg | **vitamin C** 11 mg | **vitamin A** 64 mcg.

39

the great gazpacho

1 kg (2 lb) ripe yellow tomatoes, skinned, deseeded and chopped

½ cucumber, peeled, deseeded and chopped

2 yellow peppers, cored, deseeded and chopped

2 garlic cloves, crushed

1 small onion, roughly chopped

6 basil leaves, plus extra to garnish

2 tablespoons white wine vinegar

100 ml (3½ fl oz) olive oil

300 ml (½ pint) vegetable stock

1 tablespoon lemon juice

Tabasco sauce (optional)

salt and pepper

to garnish

4 tablespoons Greek yogurt

4 tablespoons finely diced red pepper or red chillies

The vibrant colour of this delicious soup tells you that it is full of vitamin C, a natural antihistamine, making it a good anti-inflammatory choice for hayfever sufferers.

1 In a large bowl, mix together the tomatoes, cucumber, peppers, garlic, onion, basil, vinegar and olive oil and season well. Cover and leave in a cool place overnight.

2 The next day, add the stock and lemon juice and blend the mixture in a food processor until smooth. Transfer to a bowl, cover and chill.

3 Add a little Tabasco sauce if desired and season to taste. Pour the soup into chilled bowls and garnish with a spoonful of Greek yogurt, a sprinkling of red pepper or chilli and a few basil leaves.

makes 4 portions

NUTRITIONAL CONTENT: energy 280 kcals I **protein** 6 g I **fat** 24 g I **carbohydrate** 12 g I **calcium** 100 mg I **iron** 1.6 mg I **vitamin C** 103 mg.

41

NUTRITIONAL CONTENT: energy 224 kcals | **protein** 6 g | **fat** 17 g | **carbohydrate** 13 g | **calcium** 20 mg | **iron** 0.9 mg | **vitamin C** 6 mg.

375 g (12 oz) fresh wild mushrooms, such as morels, shiitake or oyster

1 tablespoon olive oil

1 onion, roughly chopped

1 potato, finely diced

1 litre (1¾ pints) chicken stock

2 garlic cloves, crushed

350 ml (12 fl oz) reduced-fat crème fraîche

salt and pepper

This healthy soup is ideal for people with high cholesterol as both mushrooms and garlic are well-known blood thinners. Shiitake mushrooms also have potent anticancer properties.

1 Chop the mushrooms very finely, reserving a few whole ones for the garnish.

2 Pour half of the oil into a heavy saucepan and cook the onion and potato gently for 10 minutes, or until the onion is translucent and the potato cooked through. Transfer to a food processor, cover with some of the stock and blend until smooth.

3 Put the chopped and whole mushrooms and garlic into the pan with the rest of the oil and sweat them gently for about 5 minutes. Add the remaining stock and bring to the boil then simmer for two minutes. Reserve the whole mushrooms.

4 Stir the potato mixture into the crème fraîche in a large bowl. Remove the soup from the heat and briskly stir a ladleful into the crème fraîche mixture. Add another couple of ladlefuls, and stir carefully. Return to the pan and mix. Replace the pan on a very low heat and reheat gently. Season to taste and serve in warmed bowls, garnished with the reserved mushrooms.

makes 4 portions

wild mushroom dream

classic c & c

1 tablespoon olive oil

2 bay leaves

1 onion, roughly chopped

2 garlic cloves, chopped

625 g (1¼ lb) carrots, roughly chopped

1 small bunch of coriander, leaves separated from stems

1.2 litres (2 pints) vegetable stock

½ teaspoon garam masala

salt and pepper

4 tablespoons Greek yogurt or soya cream, to garnish

Carrots help to kill bacteria and viruses, so are an essential immune-boosting ingredient. There is a lot to be said for the old adage that carrots help you see in the dark – they really do improve your eyesight.

1 Heat the oil in a saucepan, add the bay leaves, onion and garlic and fry for 2 minutes. Add the carrots, coriander stems and stock and bring to the boil. Simmer until the carrots are completely cooked.

2 Let the soup cool slightly, then remove the bay leaves and purée the soup in a food processor until smooth. If you like a very smooth soup, strain the soup back into the saucepan through a fine sieve; if not, just pour it all back into the pan and reheat gently. Season with salt, pepper and garam masala.

3 Finely chop half the coriander leaves and stir them into the soup. Serve the soup in warmed bowls and garnish each portion with a tablespoon of Greek yogurt swirled in and the remaining coriander leaves.

makes 4 portions

NUTRITIONAL CONTENT: energy 152 kcals | **protein** 5 g | **fat** 9 g | **carbohydrate** 17 g | **calcium** 122 mg | **iron** 1 mg | **vitamin C** 13 mg.

45

simply strawberry

875 g (1¾ lb) strawberries, hulled

75 ml (3 fl oz) orange juice

75 ml (3 fl oz) white grape juice

75 g (3 oz) clear honey

2 tablespoons cornflour

50 ml (2 fl oz) cold water

1 teaspoon lemon juice

amaretto biscuits, broken, to decorate

Strawberries are antiviral, antibacterial and full of vitamin C, and they raise the levels of antioxidants in the body. This soup is a light, immune-boosting and luxurious way to finish a meal.

1 Blend the strawberries in a food processor then pass the purée through a sieve to remove the seeds.

2 Combine the orange and grape juices, honey and sieved strawberries in a saucepan and heat gently until the honey has dissolved.

3 Mix the cornflour with the water and beat until no lumps remain. Pour into the hot soup, stirring continuously until the soup thickens. Add lemon juice to taste. Pour the soup into small bowls and decorate with the chunks of amaretto biscuits.

makes 4 portions

NUTRITIONAL CONTENT: energy 152 kcals I **calcium** 110 mg I **magnesium** 55 mg I **zinc** 1.1 mg I **vitamin C** 219 mg I **vitamin A** 183 mcg.

NUTRITIONAL CONTENT: energy 211 kcals | **calcium** 164 mg | **magnesium** 46 mg | **zinc** 1 mg | **vitamin C** 182 mg | **vitamin A** 3393 mcg.

1 orange

250 g (8 oz) carrot

125 g (4 oz) beetroot

125 g (4 oz) strawberries, hulled

ice cubes

Carrots, beetroots and oranges are all rich in vitamins A and C, antioxidants and phytonutrients such as alpha- and betacarotene. This juice is also a rich source of potassium – a real tonic.

1 Reserve a few strips of orange peel for decoration, then juice the carrot, beetroot and orange. Put the juice into a blender with a couple of ice cubes and the strawberries.

2 Blend for 20 seconds and serve in a tall glass, decorated with strips of orange rind.

makes 200 ml (7 fl oz)

power pack

NUTRITIONAL CONTENT: energy 106 kcals | calcium 125 mg | magnesium 26 mg | zinc 0.3 mg | vitamin C 133 mg | vitamin A 687 mcg.

2 oranges

1 carrot

ice cubes

A great juice to get you going in the morning, with lots of vitamin C and betacarotene. The oranges provide calcium and magnesium, vital for body-cell repair.

1 Cut a slice from one of the oranges and set aside. Remove the skin from both oranges, leaving the pith in place. Juice the carrot with the oranges and serve over ice decorated with the reserved slice of orange.

makes 200 ml (7 fl oz)

vitamin vitality

energy bubble

3 apples, preferably red, plus slices, to decorate

1 mango

2 passion fruits

ice cubes

Yellow-fleshed mango is high in betacarotene, important in preventing some cancers. The apples and passion fruit add a healthy burst of vitamin C to get that energy going.

1 Juice the apples and mango with the passion fruit. Pour the juice into a glass and add a couple of ice cubes. Decorate with apple slices.

makes 300 ml (½ pint)

NUTRITIONAL CONTENT: **energy** 249 kcals | **calcium** 33 mg | **magnesium** 43 mg | **zinc** 0.4 mg | **vitamin C** 71 mg | **vitamin A** 497 mcg.

53

red wire

100 g (3½ oz) red grapes

2 small beetroots, about 100 g (3½ oz)

2 small plums, plus wedges, to decorate

A colourful and attractive juice high in folate from the beetroot. The grapes and plums make it naturally sweet, giving an instant energy kick.

1 Juice the grapes, beetroot and plums together and serve in a tumbler over ice. Decorate with plum wedges.

makes 200 ml (7 fl oz)

NUTRITIONAL CONTENT: energy 116 kcals | **calcium** 40 mg | **magnesium** 22 mg | **zinc** 0.6 mg | **vitamin C** 10 mg | **vitamin A** 34 mcg.

bionic tonic

1 large banana

1 large ripe mango

150 g (5 oz) natural bio yogurt

300 ml (½ pint) pineapple juice

chunks of pineapple, to decorate

A scrumptious smoothie that is a small meal in itself. Yogurt supplies vital protein, calcium and magnesium, and the vitamins from the fruit make this an action-packed drink.

1 Slice the banana and roughly chop the mango flesh. Freeze for at least 2 hours or overnight.

2 Place the frozen banana and mango in a blender with the yogurt and pineapple juice. Process until smooth, pour into a glass and decorate with pineapple chunks and a stirrer.

makes 600 ml (1 pint)

NUTRITIONAL CONTENT: energy 407 kcals I **calcium** 259 mg I **magnesium** 98 mg I **zinc** 1.3 mg I **vitamin C** 103 mg I **vitamin A** 503 mcg.

smooth and soothing

40 g (1½ oz) dried cranberries, plus extra for decoration

juice of ½ lemon

1 large banana

1 tablespoon sesame seeds

2 tablespoons Greek yogurt

200 ml (7 fl oz) milk

crushed ice

This smoothie is rich in calcium (vital for bones and body cell repair) and also has useful amounts of iron (good for blood) and zinc, which is essential for healing and repair of body tissue. The yoghurt and banana make this quite a substantial drink, a small meal in itself.

1 Process the cranberries and lemon juice in a blender until the berries are finely chopped.

2 Add the banana and sesame seeds then purée, scraping the mixture down from the sides of the bowl if necessary.

3 Add the yogurt and milk, processing until smooth and frothy. Pour into a glass over crushed ice and decorate with the extra dried cranberries.

makes 300 ml (½ pint)

NUTRITIONAL CONTENT: energy 395 kcals I **calcium** 476 mg I **magnesium** 120 mg I **zinc** 2.2 mg I **vitamin C** 36 mg I **vitamin A** 174 mcg.

NUTRITIONAL CONTENT: energy 220 kcals | **calcium** 73 mg | **magnesium** 68 mg | **zinc** 0.4 mg | **vitamin C** 235 mg | **vitamin A** 1005 mcg.

250 g (8 oz) strawberries, hulled

1 kiwi fruit

½ large banana

1 tablespoon spirulina

i tablespoon linseeds

ice cubes

to decorate

1 tablespoon linseeds

1 sprig fresh redcurrants

high kick

Spirulina is a green powder made from seaweed and is high in calcium, magnesium and vitamin A to give this smoothie a really high kick.

1 Juice the strawberries and kiwi, then process the juice in a blender with the banana, spirulina, linseeds and a couple of ice cubes. Pour into a glass and decorate with redcurrants and linseeds.

makes 200 ml (7 fl oz)

NUTRITIONAL CONTENT: **energy** 95 kcals I **calcium** 81 mg I **magnesium** 28 mg I **zinc** 0.4 mg I **vitamin C** 150 mg I **vitamin A** 8 mcg.

100 g (3½ oz) strawberries, hulled

75 g (3 oz) redcurrants, plus extra to decorate

½ orange

125 ml (4 fl oz) water

½ teaspoon clear honey (optional)

crushed ice

Colourful and cleansing, this refreshing drink packs a vitamin C punch. Oranges can improve your circulation, making you feel instantly energized.

1 Juice the fruit, then add the water. Pour into a glass, stir in the honey, if using, and add some crushed ice. Decorate with the extra redcurrants.

makes 250 ml (8 fl oz)

blood orange

rose royce

100 g (3½ oz) freshly picked rosehips

200 ml (7 fl oz) boiling water

2 crisp dessert apples

to serve

rose petals

ice cubes

Wild roses provide an abundant, free supply of nutrient-rich rosehips which are packed with vitamin C, a powerful antioxidant essential for natural immunity and energy supply.

1 Blend the rosehips in a food processor until finely chopped. Turn into a small pan and add the water. Cover and simmer gently for 10 minutes, then leave to cool.

2 Juice the apples and strain the rosehip juice into the apple juice. Serve with rose petals and ice cubes.

makes 200 ml (7 fl oz)

NUTRITIONAL CONTENT: energy 40 kcals I **calcium** 5 mg I **magnesium** 7 mg I **zinc** 0.1 mg I **vitamin C** 126 mg I **vitamin A** 37 mcg.

NUTRITIONAL CONTENT: energy 147 kcals | **calcium** 71 mg | **magnesium** 39 mg | **zinc** 0.5 mg | **vitamin C** 31 mg | **vitamin A** 12 mcg.

1 large pear, preferably red

125 g (4 oz) parsnip

15 g (½ oz) fresh root ginger

125 ml (4 fl oz) sparkling water

Parsnips make a surprisingly delicious juice and mix well with fresh ginger and pears to make a drink that will provide plenty of slow-release energy.

1 Cut several long, thin slices from the pear and reserve. Roughly chop the remainder with the parsnips and ginger.

2 Push the parsnips and ginger, then the pear through the juicer. Pour over the pear slices in a tall glass and serve topped up with sparkling water.

makes 300 ml (½ pint)

energy fizz

star burst

3 whole star anise

½ teaspoon clear honey

150 ml (¼ pint) water

150 g (5 oz) cantaloupe melon

2 mandarins, or 1 small orange, peeled

Star anise has both medicinal and cosmetic uses. Its distinctive aniseed flavour blends well with melon and mandarin juice to make this refreshing, aromatic infusion with a slightly exotic touch.

1 Put the star anise and honey in a small pan with the water and bring slowly to the boil. Cover and simmer very gently for 5 minutes.

2 Cut a long wedge from the melon and reserve. Cut away the skin from the remainder and roughly chop the flesh, along with the mandarins or orange.

3 Juice the fruits and mix with the strained anise syrup in a glass. Serve warm or chilled, decorated with the melon wedge.

makes 300 ml (½ pint)

NUTRITIONAL CONTENT: energy 103 kcals I **calcium** 100 mg I **magnesium** 32 mg I **zinc** 0.3 mg I **vitamin C** 104 mg I **vitamin A** 256 mcg.

69

warm and spicy

250 g (8 oz) sweet white grapes

1 cinnamon stick

several lemon balm sprigs

When you need a hot drink, try this comforting treat instead of tea or coffee. Full of natural sweetness, it'll maintain your energy levels during a busy day, bringing with it the warm spiciness of cinnamon and fresh tang of lemon balm.

1 Juice the grapes and put the juice in a small pan with the cinnamon and most of the lemon balm. Heat without boiling and simmer gently, covered, for 4–5 minutes.

2 Lift out the lemon balm with a fork and pour the juice into a cup or glass. Serve decorated with the reserved sprig of lemon balm.

makes 200 ml (7 fl oz)

NUTRITIONAL CONTENT: energy 156 kcals I **calcium** 63 mg I **magnesium** 26 mg I **zinc** 0.3 mg I **vitamin C** 8 mg I **vitamin A** 18 mcg.

berry mull

1 vanilla pod

½ teaspoon clear honey

100 ml (3½ fl oz) water

250 g (8 oz) strawberries

150 g (5 oz) blueberries

small handful of raspberries, to decorate

Strawberries, raspberries and blueberries are packed with vitamins and minerals which help maintain good health and vitality, naturally. The vanilla infusion adds a subtle spiciness.

1 Split the vanilla pod with a knife and put in a small pan with the honey and water. Cover and simmer gently for 5 minutes then lift out the vanilla pod.

2 Juice the strawberries and blueberries. Add the juice to the pan and heat through gently. Pour over the raspberries in a large glass. Serve with a spoon, if liked.

makes 300 ml (½ pint)

NUTRITIONAL CONTENT: energy 137 kcals I **calcium** 68 mg I **magnesium** 40 mg I **zinc** 0.7 mg I **vitamin C** 230 mg I **vitamin A** 11 mcg.

lentil power

3 tablespoons vegetable oil

2 large onions, roughly chopped

4 garlic cloves, crushed

4 teaspoons cumin seeds

500 g (1 lb) dried green or brown lentils, rinsed

1 bay leaf

½ teaspoon dried oregano

3 litres (5 pints) chicken stock

to garnish

150 ml (5 fl oz) soured cream

roasted cumin seeds

Lentils are an excellent source of minerals for nearly every organ in the body. They are especially effective when you are suffering from muscular fatigue as they neutralize the excess acids produced by weary muscles.

1 Heat 2 tablespoons of the oil in a saucepan and sauté the onion, garlic and 3 teaspoons of the cumin seeds for about 5 minutes, letting the onion brown and the cumin roast slightly. Add the lentils, bay leaf, oregano and stock. Bring to the boil and simmer for about 35 minutes, or until the lentils are soft.

2 Remove the bay leaf, and purée the soup in a food processor. Blend all of the soup if you like a smooth texture, or if you prefer your soups a little chunkier, blend only half of it then stir this back into the unblended part.

3 Heat the remaining oil in a small pan and sauté the remaining cumin seeds over a medium heat for about 1 minute, or until they are slightly crisp. Drain on kitchen paper. Serve the soup in warmed bowls garnished with a tablespoon of soured cream swirled over and the roasted cumin seeds sprinkled over.

makes 10 portions

NUTRITIONAL CONTENT: energy 233 kcals I **protein** 14 mg I **fat** 8 mg I **carbohydrate** 29 mg I **calcium** 73 mg I **iron** 6 mg I **vitamin C** 3 mg.

NUTRITIONAL CONTENT: energy 284 kcals | **protein** 4 mg | **fat** 17 mg | **carbohydrate** 32 mg | **calcium** 49 mg | **iron** 2.4 mg | **vitamin C** 33 mg.

1 tablespoon olive oil

1 onion, roughly chopped

2 garlic cloves, crushed

1 teaspoon finely grated fresh root ginger

1 teaspoon medium curry powder

500 g (1 lb) sweet potato, peeled and diced

1 litre (1¾ pints) vegetable or chicken stock

salt and pepper

coconut and lime cream

150 ml (¼ pint) coconut cream

juice of ½ lime

1 teaspoon grated lime rind

Sweet potato is the richest low-fat source of vitamin E, which is vital for energy production and cellular respiration. It contributes to heart health and is a good source of dietary antioxidants, particularly betacarotene. It can help to lower high blood pressure and also helps anaemia. It may also protect against inflammatory conditions and is attributed with anti-ageing properties.

1 Heat the oil in a large saucepan over a medium heat and sauté the onion, garlic, ginger and curry powder until the onion is translucent. Add the sweet potato and cook for 1–2 minutes without browning it.

2 Add the stock, cover and cook for 10 minutes, or until the sweet potato is tender. Purée the soup in a food processor then return it to the pan and gently reheat. Season to taste.

3 To make the coconut and lime cream, mix together the coconut cream, lime juice and lime rind. Ladle the soup into bowls and garnish with a generous drizzle of the cream.

makes 4 portions

caribbean spice

black bean bonanza

200 g (7 oz) dried black-eyed beans, soaked in water overnight

3 tablespoons olive oil

1 onion, finely chopped

1 garlic clove, crushed

2 litres (3½ pints) vegetable stock

1 celery stick, sliced

1 large carrot, sliced

2 thyme sprigs

2 bay leaves

a pinch each of ground cloves and mace

salt and pepper

to garnish

2 chillies, deseeded and finely diced

1 tablespoon chopped coriander leaves

This robust soup is packed with fibre and is very good for cleansing the digestive tract. Beans are excellent for sustained energy and have a cholesterol-lowering effect on the bloodstream.

1 Drain and rinse the beans three times and allow to dry. Put the olive oil, onion and garlic in a large saucepan and sweat gently, covered, for about 5 minutes.

2 Add the beans and stock and bring to the boil then reduce the heat to a simmer. Add the celery, carrot, thyme, bay leaves, cloves and mace and cook for 1½ hours, or until the beans are soft.

3 Let the mixture cool slightly, discard the herbs, then purée in a food processor or blender until smooth. Return the soup to the pan and reheat it, then season with salt and pepper. Serve in warm bowls with a sprinkling of chillies and coriander.

makes 6 portions

NUTRITIONAL CONTENT: energy 192 kcals I **protein** 9 mg I **fat** 8 mg I **carbohydrate** 22 mg I **calcium** 50 mg I **iron** 3 mg I **vitamin C** 8 mg.

hot stuff

300 g (10 oz) tomatoes

100 g (3½ oz) celery, plus slivers, to decorate

2.5 cm (1 inch) cube of fresh root ginger, roughly chopped

1 garlic clove

2.5 cm (1 inch) cube of fresh horseradish

175 g (6 oz) carrot

ice cubes

This juice is good for bronchitis. Tomatoes and carrots provide large amounts of vitamin C, while garlic, ginger and horseradish are all-powerful antioxidants – imperative for fighting off infections. Combined, they also deal a mighty anti-mucus punch.

1 Juice all the ingredients, blend with 2 ice cubes and serve in a tumbler. Decorate with celery slivers.

makes 150 ml (¼ pint)

NUTRITIONAL CONTENT: **energy** 130 kcals **| calcium** 119 mg **| magnesium** 36 mg **| zinc** 0.8 mg **| vitamin C** 32 mg **| vitamin A** 2696 mcg.

81

belly berry

250 g (8 oz) apple

125 g (4 oz) blueberries, fresh or frozen

Apples and blueberries are both great for settling stomach upsets and combatting digestive disorders,

1 Juice the apple, then process in a blender or food processor with the blueberries. Serve in a tumbler over ice, if liked, and with a straw.

makes 150 ml (¼ pint)

NUTRITIONAL CONTENT: **energy** 166 kcals I **calcium** 26 mg I **magnesium** 19 mg I **zinc** 0.5 mg I **vitamin C** 36 mg I **vitamin A** 14 mcg.

NUTRITIONAL CONTENT: **energy** 171 kcals | **calcium** 260 mg | **magnesium** 92 mg | **zinc** 1.3 mg | **vitamin C** 48 mg | **vitamin A** 760 mcg.

250 g (8 oz) pear, plus slices, to decorate

25 g (1 oz) pitted prunes

125 g (4 oz) spinach

ice cubes

This combination of fruit and vegetables is rich in fibre, with good cleansing properties to stimulate the abdomen and improve digestion. This juice really could be called a lethal weapon – a dose of three potent laxatives to relieve constipation.

1 Juice all the ingredients together and serve in a glass over ice cubes. Decorate with the extra pear slices and serve with a stirrer.

makes 200 ml (7 fl oz)

way to go

lounge lizard

250 g (8 oz) kiwi fruit

125 g (4 oz) cucumber

1 tablespoon pomegranate seeds (if available)

slices of lime, to decorate

The vitamin C and potassium-rich ingredients in this juice help to lower blood pressure.

1 Wash the kiwi fruits and cucumber but do not peel them.

2 Juice both and serve with slices of lime. Stir in a tablespoon of pomegranate seeds, if available.

makes 150 ml (½ pint)

NUTRITIONAL CONTENT: energy 143 kcals I **calcium** 37 mg I **magnesium** 49 mg I **zinc** 0.4 mg I **vitamin C** 162 mg I **vitamin A** 29 mcg.

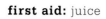

twister

125 g (4 oz) pink grapefruit, plus slices, to decorate

125 g (4 oz) carrot

125 g (4 oz) spinach

ice cubes

This juice is beneficial to arthritis sufferers. The salicylic acid in grapefruit works to break down uric acid deposits and the carrot and spinach help to rebuild and regenerate cartilage and joints.

1 Peel the grapefruit, keeping as much of the pith as possible. Juice all the ingredients and serve over ice in a tumbler. Decorate with slices of grapefruit.

makes 200 ml (7 fl oz)

NUTRITIONAL CONTENT: energy 106 kcals **| calcium** 284 mg **| magnesium** 90 mg **| zinc** 1.1 mg **| vitamin C** 83 mg **| vitamin A** 1860 mcg.

hula kula

½ **pineapple, peeled and roughly chopped**

100 ml (3½ fl oz) **coconut milk**

100 ml (3½ fl oz) **soya milk**

pineapple leaf, to decorate

A tropical smoothie that uses pineapple to aid digestion. Choose a soya milk enriched with calcium and vitamins to make the nutritional content even better.

1 Place all the ingredients in a blender with some ice cubes and blend until the mixture is smooth. Decorate with pineapple leaves.

makes 300 ml (½ pint)

NUTRITIONAL CONTENT: energy 142 kcals I **calcium** 80 mg I **magnesium** 79 mg I **zinc** 0.5 mg I **vitamin C** 28 mg I **vitamin A** 6 mcg.

sweet chariot

¼ **pineapple, peeled and roughly chopped**

100 g (3½ oz) grapes

1 small orange, plus wedges, to decorate

1 small apple

½ **large mango, peeled**

½ **large banana, peeled**

ice cubes

mint leaves, cut into strips, to decorate

A mini-meal in a glass, this smoothie is high in calcium, magnesium and phosphorus, all essential for protecting bones and maintaining body cells. There's also a high vitamin C content, for fighting infection and viruses.

1 Juice the pineapple, grapes, orange and apple. Process in a blender with the mango, banana and a couple of ice cubes. Serve decorated with orange wedges and strips of mint.

makes 400 ml (14 fl oz)

NUTRITIONAL CONTENT: **energy** 227 kcals I **calcium** 103 mg I **magnesium** 69 mg I **zinc** 0.6 mg I **vitamin C** 118 mg I **vitamin A** 241 mcg.

passion thriller

½ Galia or honeydew melon, skinned

125 g (4 oz) cucumber

1 small avocado, peeled and stoned

50 g (2 oz) dried apricots, plus slivers, to decorate

1 tablespoon wheatgerm

ice cubes

A cool-looking smoothie high in vitamin E (great for smooth skin). It also contains selenium, an essential trace mineral for blood formation.

1 Juice the melon and cucumber. Process in a blender with the avocado, apricots, wheatgerm and a couple of ice cubes. Decorate with dried apricot slivers.

makes 200 ml (7 fl oz)

NUTRITIONAL CONTENT: energy 343 kcals | **calcium** 98 mg | **magnesium** 96 mg | **zinc** 1.9 mg | **vitamin C** 27 mg | **vitamin A** 68 mcg.

acher shaker

100 g (3½ oz) strawberries, hulled

½ pineapple, plus wedges, to decorate

1 banana, peeled

ice cubes

Plenty of fruit and vegetables can help keep arthritic pains at bay. The high vitamin C content of this drink makes it a great pick-me-up.

1 Juice the strawberries and pineapple. Pour the juice into a blender, add the banana and a couple of ice cubes and process. Serve with a spoon and decorated with a couple of pineapple wedges and a stirrer.

makes 300 ml (½ pint)

NUTRITIONAL CONTENT: energy 206 kcals ǀ **calcium** 66 mg ǀ **magnesium** 77 mg ǀ **zinc** 0.5 mg ǀ **vitamin C** 116 mg ǀ **vitamin A** 12 mcg.

NUTRITIONAL CONTENT: **energy** 173 kcals | **calcium** 211 mg | **magnesium** 90 mg | **zinc** 0.8 mg | **vitamin C** 140 mg | **vitamin A** 86 mcg.

2 grapefruits

750 g (1½ lb) cucumber, plus slices, to decorate

1 lemon, plus slices, to decorate

sparkling mineral water

mint leaves, to decorate

ice cubes

A cooling drink to savour on a hot day. Like most citrus fruits, grapefruit is a good source of calcium, essential for the maintenance of strong bones, as well as being rich in vitamin C.

1 Juice the grapefruit, cucumber and lemon. Pour into a jug over ice, and top up with sparkling mineral water to make up to 400 ml (14 fl oz). Decorate with mint leaves and slices of cucumber and lemon.

makes 400 ml (14 fl oz)

karma kooler

zesty ginger beer

25 g (1 oz) fresh root ginger

1 lime

boiling water

2 tablespoons clear honey

150 ml (¼ pint) sparkling water

Ginger is one of the best healing foods available, great for relieving stomach upsets, indigestion and nausea and for clearing the sinuses. It also gets the circulation going and soothes the pain of arthritis, so it's definitely an ingredient worth some space in the refrigerator.

1 Finely grate the ginger into a measuring jug, then scrape the pulp left on the grater into the jug. Grate the lime rind and add to the ginger. Make up to 100 ml (3½ fl oz) with boiling water and leave to stand for 10 minutes.

2 Strain into a tall glass and stir in the honey and squeeze in the lime juice. Chill the juice if you like an ice cold drink and serve topped up with sparkling water.

makes 300 ml (½ pint)

NUTRITIONAL CONTENT: energy 158 kcals I **calcium** 10 mg I **magnesium** 3 mg I **zinc** 0.5 mg I **vitamin C** 12 mg I **vitamin A** 3 mcg.

101

NUTRITIONAL CONTENT: energy 137 kcals | **calcium** 60 mg | **magnesium** 29 mg | **zinc** 1 mg | **vitamin C** 14 mg | **vitamin A** 29 mcg.

100 g (3½ oz) beetroot
½ small fennel bulb
150 g (5 oz) black or red grapes
crushed ice

These vegetables are a real powerhouse of goodness, brilliant as a general pick-me-up if you're feeling lethargic, dehydrated or simply hungover. Juiced beetroot is surprisingly sweet so you might want to add a squeeze of lemon juice as well.

1 Roughly chop the beetroot and fennel and push through the juicer along with the grapes. Pour over crushed ice in a tall glass and serve immediately.

makes 200 ml (7 fl oz)

beet this

tummy tonic

5 cardamom pods

good pinch of cumin seeds

3 mint sprigs, plus extra leaves, to decorate

1 green tea bag

200 ml (7 fl oz) boiling water

honey, to taste

Mint is a vital ingredient in natural remedies, particularly as an aid to digestion. Cardamom pods are also good for the digestive system and along with the cumin turn this into a deliciously spicy, aromatic blend.

1 Lightly crush the cardamon pods and cumin seeds using a pestle and mortar. Add the mint sprigs and bruise the leaves to release the flavour. Turn them into a small jug or teapot along with the teabag and make up to 200 ml (7 fl oz) with the boiling water.

2 Leave to infuse for 4 minutes then strain into a cup. Add a little honey to taste and serve decorated with extra mint leaves.

makes 200 ml (7 fl oz)

NUTRITIONAL CONTENT: energy 24 kcals | calcium 36 mg | magnesium 11 mg | zinc 0.2 mg | vitamin C 1 mg | vitamin A 6 mcg.

fever fusion

4 large feverfew sprigs

3–4 fresh or dried hibiscus flowers

pared strip of lemon rind

200 ml (7 fl oz) boiling water

1 teaspoon lemon juice

clear honey, to taste

Feverfew is renowned as a cure for headaches and fever, hence its name. In herbal medicine it's still widely used as a treatment for migraines, because of its ability to improve blood vessel functioning and reduce inflammation. Both flowers and leaves can be used.

1 Put 3 of the feverfew sprigs, the hibiscus and lemon rind in a cup and add the boiling water. Leave to infuse for 4–5 minutes. Lift out the herbs and lemon rind and stir in the lemon juice and a little honey, to taste. Decorate with the remaining sprig of feverfew.

makes 200 ml (7 fl oz)

NUTRITIONAL CONTENT: energy 14 kcals I **calcium** 7 mg I **magnesium** 3 mg I **zinc** trace I **vitamin C** 4 mg I **vitamin A** 0 mcg.

107

c for comfort

150 g (5 oz) blackcurrants

3 thyme sprigs

200 ml (7 fl oz) boiling water

clear honey, to taste

Sore throats and coughs can really benefit from a dose of this comforting tea. Blackcurrants are rich in vitamin C and give a vital boost to the body's own natural defences. Fresh thyme has antiseptic properties and, combined with the honey, eases any discomfort.

1 Tip the blackcurrants into a bowl and add the thyme and boiling water. Using a fork, mash the blackcurrants against the side of the bowl to release all the juices.

2 Leave for 2 minutes then strain into a warmed cup. Add a little honey to taste.

makes 300 ml (½ pint)

NUTRITIONAL CONTENT: energy 54 kcals I **calcium** 90 mg I **magnesium** 26 mg I **zinc** 0.5 mg I **vitamin C** 300 mg I **vitamin A** 25 mcg.

109

NUTRITIONAL CONTENT: energy 250 kcals | protein 29 g | fat 12 g | carbohydrate 7 g | calcium 330 mg | iron 3 mg | vitamin C 24 mg.

500 g (1 lb) asparagus

2 tablespoons olive oil

125 g (4 oz) celery, sliced

125 g (4 oz) leeks, sliced

125 g (4 oz) onions, sliced

1.2 litres (2 pints) chicken stock

200 g (7 oz) silken tofu

300 g (10 oz) cooked chicken, cut into bite-sized pieces

1 teaspoon chopped thyme

salt and pepper

2 tablespoons chopped tarragon, to garnish

This soup is high in protein, low in carbohydrates and contains only healthy fat. It is an excellent choice for a low carbohydrate diet. If you are recovering from an illness the powerful combination of healthy protein and calcium will aid a speedy recovery.

1 Trim the bottoms of the asparagus stalks where they begin to turn white. Cut off the tips about 3.5 cm (1½ inches) from the top and set aside. Roughly slice the remaining sections.

2 Heat the oil in a large saucepan, add the celery, leeks and onions and fry until soft. Add the stock and bring to the boil. Add the sliced asparagus and simmer for 5 minutes. Remove the soup from the heat and blend in a food processor with the tofu.

3 Return the soup to the pan and season with salt and pepper. Add the asparagus tips, chicken pieces and thyme and simmer for 10 minutes. Pour into warm serving bowls and sprinkle with chopped tarragon.

makes 4 portions

recovery

chill-out

1 garlic bulb, skin left on

125 g (4 oz) fresh white breadcrumbs

1 litre (1¾ pints) chicken or vegetable stock

125 g (4 oz) blanched almonds, lightly toasted

5 tablespoons olive oil

1½ tablespoons sherry vinegar

salt and pepper

to garnish

2 oranges, segmented

halved black and white grapes

toasted almonds

handful of coriander and mint leaves

Almonds contain phosphorus and magnesium, both crucial for strong bones, so this soup can reduce the risk or effects of osteoporosis. Nuts are also known to reduce levels of LDL (bad cholesterol). Garlic is a powerful blood thinner and general circulatory tonic.

1 Roast the garlic bulb in a preheated oven at 180°C (350°F), Gas Mark 4, for about 30 minutes until soft. Meanwhile, soak the breadcrumbs in 150 ml (¼ pint) of the stock for 5 minutes.

2 Remove the garlic from the oven and let it cool, then squeeze the pulp into the bread mixture. Blend the almonds in a food processor until finely ground. Add the bread mixture to the almonds and blend. Gradually add the oil until it forms a smooth paste, then add the remainder of the stock and the sherry vinegar and process until smooth.

3 Transfer the soup to a bowl and season with salt and pepper. Cover and chill for at least 2–3 hours. Serve the soup in chilled bowls garnished with orange segments, grapes, toasted almonds, coriander and mint.

makes 6 portions

NUTRITIONAL CONTENT: energy 287 kcals I **protein** 7 g I **fat** 22 g I **carbohydrate** 17 g I **calcium** 96 mg I **iron** 1.2 mg I **vitamin C** 23 mg.

113

fiery indian broth

50 g (2 oz) butter

1 large onion, chopped

3 garlic cloves, chopped

1 teaspoon cumin seeds

1 teaspoon ground coriander

pinch of ground cinnamon

pinch of ground nutmeg

1 teaspoon chopped fresh root ginger

½ teaspoon ground cloves

1 red chilli, deseeded and finely chopped

½ teaspoon ground cardamom

200 g (7 oz) dried green lentils

1.2 litres (2 pints) vegetable stock

500 g (1 lb) spinach

250 g (8 oz) Greek yogurt

salt and pepper

The staples of Indian cuisine are recommended by health professionals to prevent heart disease, obesity, cancer, diabetes and stroke. Lentils are little vitamin pills – full of B vitamins – and good for energy production. Dry skin benefits from the vitamin B2 in both the lentils and yogurt, which is also good for digestion.

1 Melt the butter in a large heavy saucepan, add the onion, garlic, cumin, coriander, cinnamon, nutmeg, ginger, cloves, chilli and cardamom and fry for 5 minutes.

2 Add the lentils and stir for about 2 minutes. Pour in the stock, bring to the boil and simmer, covered, for 1 hour.

3 Chop the spinach finely, add it to the broth and simmer for 5 minutes. Stir in the yogurt, season with salt and pepper and heat through gently for 1 minute. Serve the soup in warmed bowls or mugs.

makes 6 portions

NUTRITIONAL CONTENT: energy 257 kcals | protein 14 g | fat 13 g | carbohydrate 23 g | calcium 260 mg | iron 6.6 mg | vitamin C 26 mg.

sour power

1 pomegranate

1 carrot

100 g (3½ oz) grapes

crushed ice

The tangy taste of pomegranate enlivens this cleansing drink, which is high in protective carotenes.

1 Scoop out the pomegranate pulp and seeds. Reserve a few seeds for decoration, then juice the pulp and the rest of the seeds with the carrot and grapes. Serve over crushed ice mixed with the reserved pomegranate seeds.

makes 200 ml (7 fl oz)

NUTRITIONAL CONTENT: energy 117 kcals I **calcium** 36 mg I **magnesium** 17 mg I **zinc** 0.4 mg I **vitamin C** 16 mg I **vitamin A** 818 mcg.

NUTRITIONAL CONTENT: **energy** 86 kcals I **calcium** 30 mg I **magnesium** 23 mg I **zinc** 0.2 mg I **vitamin C** 72 mg I **vitamin A** 42 mcg.

1 peach

2 plums, plus wedges, to decorate

1 kiwi fruit

ice cubes

This juice is rich in betacarotenes from the peaches and plums, and high in potassium, which is good for regulating blood pressure. Plum juice stimulates bowel action, preventing the discomfort of constipation.

1 Juice all the ingredients together and serve over ice cubes. Decorate with plum wedges.

makes 200 ml (7 fl oz)

plum punch

purple passion

250 g (8 oz) blueberries

½ grapefruit

2 large apples

2.5 cm (1 inch) cube of fresh root ginger, plus thin strips, to decorate

The combination of these three fruits, plus the zest of ginger, makes this a great drink for clearing the system and warding off infection.

1 Juice all the ingredients together and serve in a tall glass with ice cubes. Decorate with thin strips of ginger.

makes 200 ml (7 fl oz)

NUTRITIONAL CONTENT: energy 247 kcals I **calcium** 63 mg I **magnesium** 35 mg I **zinc** 0.8 mg I **vitamin C** 90 mg I **vitamin A** 25 mcg.

121

bumpy ride

2 small apples, plus slices, to decorate

50 g (2 oz) beetroot

2 celery sticks

ice cubes

Beetroot is rich in folate, important for blood and for the nervous system. The high fluid content is ideal for first thing in the morning.

1 Juice all the ingredients together and serve in a tumbler over ice. Decorate with apple slices and serve with a straw.

makes 150 ml (¼ pint)

NUTRITIONAL CONTENT: energy 85 kcals | **calcium** 40 mg | **magnesium** 15 mg | **zinc** 0.4 mg | **vitamin C** 15 mg | **vitamin A** 11 mcg.

123

papaya flyer

½ **large pear, plus slices,
to decorate**

1 carrot

¼ **papaya, peeled and deseeded**

1 ice cube

This delicious juice is rich in vitamin C and betacarotene. The natural sweetness of pear, carrot and papaya will give an instant energy kick first thing in the morning, or indeed at any time of the day.

1 Juice the pear and carrot and put in a blender with the papaya and an ice cube and blend until smooth. Decorate with thin slices of pear.

makes 200 ml (7 fl oz)

NUTRITIONAL CONTENT: **energy** 145 kcals I **calcium** 70 mg I **magnesium** 23 mg I **zinc** 0.8 mg I **vitamin C** 115 mg I **vitamin A** 1386 mcg.

125

NUTRITIONAL CONTENT: energy 128 kcals I **calcium** 66 mg I **magnesium** 61 mg I **zinc** 1.3 mg I **vitamin C** 18 mg I **vitamin A** 21 mcg.

¼ **pineapple**

1 small apple

100 g (3½ oz) alfalfa sprouts

100 ml (3½ fl oz) soya milk

ice cubes

Alfalfa sprouts contain folate, magnesium, zinc and phosphorus, all essential for the formation, repair and healing of body tissue. This is a great all-round drink.

1 Juice the pineapple, apple and alfalfa sprouts together. Pour the juice into a blender with the soya milk and an ice cube and blend. Serve over ice cubes with a straw.

makes 300 ml (½ pint)

full tank

berry nice

2 bananas, peeled

200 g (7 oz) raspberries, plus extra to decorate

125 g (4 oz) blueberries, plus extra, to decorate

1 small glass of unsweetened cranberry juice

2 tablespoons natural yogurt

Packed with energy and vitamin C, as well as calcium and magnesium which are necessary for cell repair, this colourful smoothie makes a tangy and healthy start to anyone's day.

1 Roughly chop the bananas and put into a blender. Add the berries and pour in the cranberry juice. Add the yogurt and blend until smooth. Pour into a glass and decorate with the extra blueberries and raspberries.

makes 300 ml (½ pint)

NUTRITIONAL CONTENT: energy 333 kcals I **calcium** 227 mg I **magnesium** 114 mg I **zinc** 1.7 mg I **vitamin C** 134 mg I **vitamin A** 21 mcg.

green dream

2 large apples

1 celery stick

½ kiwi fruit, plus a slice, to decorate

½ lemon

1 small avocado

This smoothie is refreshing, cleansing and instantly invigorating, with a high vitamin E content to promote lovely smooth skin.

1 Juice the apple, celery, kiwi and lemon. Transfer to a blender and process with the avocado for 20 seconds to make a refreshing smoothie. Decorate with kiwi slices.

makes 200 ml (7 fl oz)

NUTRITIONAL CONTENT: energy 352 kcals | **calcium** 45 mg | **magnesium** 48 mg | **zinc** 0.8 mg | **vitamin C** 53 mg | **vitamin A** 17 mcg.

NUTRITIONAL CONTENT: **energy** 311 kcals I **calcium** 263 mg I **magnesium** 64 mg I **zinc** 2.1 mg I **vitamin C** 22 mg I **vitamin A** 13 mcg.

50 g (2 oz) shelled pecan nuts

250 g (8 oz) natural yogurt

300 ml (½ pint) apple juice

clear honey, to taste

ice cubes

Rich in calcium and magnesium for the protection of bone and cell tissue, this drink also contains pecan nuts and is packed with protein to set you up for the day.

1 Put the pecans into a food processor or blender with a few tablespoons of the yogurt and process to a paste.

2 Add the remaining yogurt and the apple juice and process again until well mixed. Sweeten to taste with honey and serve over ice.

makes 575 ml (18 fl oz)

pecan punch

fruity filler

6 ready-to-eat dried apricots

50 g (2 oz) raisins

25 g (1 oz) shelled pistachio nuts

250 ml (8 fl oz) coconut milk

250 ml (8 fl oz) apricot juice

sugar, to taste

ice cubes

Apricots and raisins are rich in potassium, good for blood pressure control, and pistachio nuts provide selenium, which is good for the blood. Altogether a power-packed smoothie, this drink is great as an occasional meal replacement.

1 Place the dried apricots, raisins and pistachios in a food processor or blender with a little of the coconut milk and process for 1 minute to make a smooth paste.

2 Add the remaining coconut milk and the apricot juice and process until will mixed. Add sugar to taste, drizzle a little coconut milk over the top and serve over ice.

makes 575 ml (18 fl oz)

NUTRITIONAL CONTENT: energy 555 kcals | **calcium** 153 mg | **magnesium** 108 mg | **zinc** 0.7 mg | **vitamin C** 65 mg | **vitamin A** 56 mcg.

cool and cleansing

1 large apple

75 g (3 oz) blackberries

150 ml (¼ pint) water

ice cubes

Keep some blackberries in the freezer to make this cleansing drink in winter or summer. It tastes good, and provides vitamins C and E.

1 Juice the apple and blackberries together then stir in the water. Pour into a glass and add a couple of ice cubes to chill. Serve with a stirrer.

makes 300 ml (½ pint)

NUTRITIONAL CONTENT: energy 66 kcals | **calcium** 35 mg | **magnesium** 22 mg | **zinc** 0.3 mg | **vitamin C** 17 mg | **vitamin A** 13 mcg.

tropicana

1 small ripe mango

2 passion fruits

juice of 1 lime

100 ml (3½ fl oz) natural yogurt

ice cubes

Mango is packed with vitamin C and betacarotene and provides a good dose of slow-release energy. A ripe mango blends to a deliciously thick consistency, and is perfect for a breakfast substitute.

1 Halve the mango, either side of the flat stone. Scoop all the flesh into a blender, discarding the skin. Halve the passion fruits and scoop the pulp into the blender.

2 Add the lime juice and yogurt and blend until smooth, scraping the mixture down from the sides of the blender if necessary. Pour over crushed ice in a tall glass.

makes 300 ml (½ pint)

NUTRITIONAL CONTENT: energy 155 kcals I **calcium** 214 mg I **magnesium** 49 mg I **zinc** 1 mg I **vitamin C** 73 mg I **vitamin A** 497 mcg.

NUTRITIONAL CONTENT: **energy** 209 kcals I **calcium** 105 mg I **magnesium** 42 mg I **zinc** 0.6 mg I **vitamin C** 148 mg I **vitamin A** 13 mcg.

1 pomelo

1 red grapefruit

100 ml (3½ fl oz) soya milk

2–3 teaspoons honey

ice cubes

This frothy pink cooler is light on calories and packed with invigorating nutrients. Sweet pomelo and red grapefruit go together to make an interesting drink but you could use two yellow grapefruits instead.

1 First squeeze the juice from the pomelo and grapefruit. To extract maximum juice from large citrus fruits, cut away the thick skins, chop the flesh and push it through a juicer.

2 Mix the juice in a bowl with the soya milk and honey. Blend with an electric whisk until a thick froth forms on the surface. Pour into a glass and serve with ice cubes.

makes 200 ml (7 fl oz)

citrus squeeze

ginger spice

300 g (10 oz) carrot

50 g (2 oz) fennel, plus strips and fronds, to serve

75 g (3 oz) celery

2.5 cm (1 inch) cube fresh root ginger, roughly chopped

1 tablespoon spirulina (optional)

ice cubes

Drink a glass of this juice before a light lunch to give you an instant energy boost and banish the dieting blues.

1 Juice the ingredients and serve over ice, with fennel fronds mixed in. You can also add 1 tablespoon of spirulina, which contains phenylalanine, to fill you up. If liked, decorate with strips of fennel.

makes 200 ml (7 fl oz)

NUTRITIONAL CONTENT: energy 183 kcals I **potassium** 1627 mg I **magnesium** 80 mg I **vitamin C** 43 mg I **vitamin A** 25,380 mcg.

143

tongue tingler

3 mint sprigs, plus extra, to decorate

½ orange

200 ml (7 fl oz) boiling water

1 passion fruit

1–2 teaspoons clear honey

An infusion releases a burst of flavour from even the smallest sprig of mint. Mixed with vitamin-packed orange and passion fruit, this tingling tea will set you off to a good start.

1 Crush the mint between your fingers to bruise it, then put it in a cup. Pare a strip of rind from the orange and add to the cup with the boiling water. Leave for 3–4 minutes then lift out the mint sprigs.

2 Halve the passion fruit and press the pulp through a tea strainer set over the cup, to extract the juice. Squeeze the orange juice and add to the cup with honey to taste. Stir well and serve with extra mint sprigs.

makes 300 ml (½ pint)

NUTRITIONAL CONTENT: energy 70 kcals **| calcium** 44 mg **| magnesium** 13 mg **| zinc** 0.3 mg **| vitamin C** 47 mg **| vitamin A** 25 mcg.

145

cleansing cranberry

1 cinnamon stick

15 g (½ oz) fresh root ginger, thinly sliced

100 ml (3½ fl oz) water

200 g (7 oz) cranberries

1 small dessert apple, roughly chopped

3–4 teaspoons clear honey

Cranberries are rich in vitamin C and among the most cleansing of fruits, warding off bacteria and viruses. Tangy and refreshing, this is a great infusion to kick start the day.

1 Cut the cinnamon stick into two and set one half aside. Break the other half into small pieces and heat it together with the ginger and water in a small pan. Heat gently without boiling for 5 minutes then leave to cool.

2 Juice the cranberries and apple. Strain the liquid in the pan into the fruit juice, then return to the cleaned pan with the honey. Heat through until the honey has dissolved and pour into a cup to serve. Serve with the reserved piece of cinnamon stick as a stirrer.

makes 200 ml (7 fl oz)

NUTRITIONAL CONTENT: energy 103 kcals I **calcium** 30 mg I **magnesium** 18 mg I **zinc** 0.6 mg I **vitamin C** 30 mg I **vitamin A** 11 mcg.

147

berried treasure

8 cloves

200 ml (7 fl oz) boiling water

100 g (3½ oz) raspberries, plus extra, to decorate

1–2 teaspoons honey

Try this infusion if you need a warming boost. It is at its best when raspberries are at their sweetest and juiciest. Cloves add a warm spiciness, but don't use too many as they will overpower the fruit.

1 Put the cloves in a small bowl and add half the boiling water. Leave for 5 minutes.

2 Mash the raspberries in a separate bowl and add the remaining boiling water. Lift out the cloves from the infused water and press the raspberry pulp through a sieve into the bowl. Stir, pour into a warmed cup and stir in the honey to taste. Decorate with the extra raspberries.

makes 250 ml (8 fl oz)

NUTRITIONAL CONTENT: energy 48 kcals | **calcium** 25 mg | **magnesium** 19 mg | **zinc** 0.4 mg | **vitamin C** 32 mg | **vitamin A** 1 mcg.

NUTRITIONAL CONTENT: energy 246 kcals | protein 8 g | fat 10 g | carbohydrate 32 g | calcium 93 mg | iron 2.6 mg | vitamin C 66 mg.

1 tablespoon olive oil

25 g (1 oz) butter

1 onion, finely chopped

1 leek, finely chopped

1 celery stick, finely chopped

3 garlic cloves, chopped

2 carrots, sliced

250 g (8 oz) squash, peeled and diced

175 g (6 oz) potatoes, peeled and diced

1 litre (1¾ pints) vegetable stock

175 g (6 oz) broccoli florets

125 g (4 oz) defrosted frozen sweetcorn kernels

200 g (7 oz) canned tomatoes

150 ml (5 fl oz) soya milk

salt and pepper

basil leaves, to garnish

Full of immune-boosting antioxidants, this chowder is the perfect antidote to cold winter weather. If you feel a cold on the way, add a few extra garlic cloves. Don't overcook the soup or you will destroy the nutrients.

1 Heat the oil and butter in a large heavy saucepan, add the onion, leek, celery and garlic and cook gently until softened. Add the carrots, squash and potatoes and stir for about 5 minutes. Add the stock, cover and cook for 10 minutes.

2 Add the broccoli, sweetcorn and tomatoes and cook for 5 minutes. Remove from the heat and allow to cool slightly. Stir in the soya milk and season to taste.

3 Put the soup into a food processor and blend to a rough purée. Pour the soup back into the pan and gently reheat. Serve in warm bowls, scattered with basil leaves.

makes 4 portions

chunky chowder

brain booster

2 teaspoons olive oil

1 teaspoon sesame oil

2 garlic cloves, finely chopped

2.5 cm (1 inch) piece of fresh root ginger, peeled and chopped

2 spring onions, finely chopped

1 red chilli, deseeded and finely chopped

1 lemongrass stalk

2 kaffir lime leaves

1 tablespoon lemon juice

2 teaspoons ground coriander

750 ml (1¼ pints) chicken stock

500 g (1 lb) papaya, peeled, deseeded and diced

250 g (8 oz) silken tofu, diced

2 tablespoons coconut milk

to garnish

thin strips of red pepper

2 tablespoons coriander leaves

This fragrant soup is a satisfying meal in a bowl. Papaya aids digestion, while tofu rebalances hormones and lowers LDL (bad cholesterol). This soup is rich in calcium, which maintains healthy bones and teeth. Vegetable stock may be used instead of chicken stock.

1 Heat the olive oil in a saucepan with the sesame oil and sauté the garlic, ginger and half the spring onion until soft. Add the chilli and cook for 1 more minute. Add the lemongrass and lime leaves, the lemon juice and ground coriander. Stir in the stock and papaya and simmer for 15 minutes.

2 Strain the soup through a fine sieve into a clean saucepan. Push it through with a wooden spoon to ensure all the papaya pulp goes through.

3 Add the tofu and cook for 5 minutes then stir in the coconut milk. Serve the soup hot or cold with the remaining spring onion, the red pepper and coriander leaves, which should be chopped at the last minute.

makes 4 portions

NUTRITIONAL CONTENT: energy 178 kcals | **protein** 7 g | **fat** 10 g | **carbohydrate** 17 g | **calcium** 370 mg | **iron** 2.2 mg | **vitamin C** 99 mg.

evergreen

50 g (2 oz) celery

50 g (2 oz) fennel

125 g (4 oz) Romaine lettuce

175 g (6 oz) pineapple

1 teaspoon chopped tarragon, plus extra sprigs to decorate

ice cubes

This juice combines celery and fennel, which help the body to utilize magnesium, and calcium which calms the nerves. With the added sedative effect of the lettuce, this drink makes an ideal stress-buster.

1 Juice the celery, fennel, lettuce, pineapple and chopped tarragon and whizz in a blender or food processor with 2 ice cubes. Serve in a tall glass and decorate with a stirrer and tarragon sprigs.

makes 200 ml (7 fl oz)

NUTRITIONAL CONTENT: energy 101 kcals I **calcium** 108 mg I **magnesium** 45 mg I **zinc** 0.8 mg I **vitamin C** 34 mg I **vitamin A** 98 mcg.

155

156

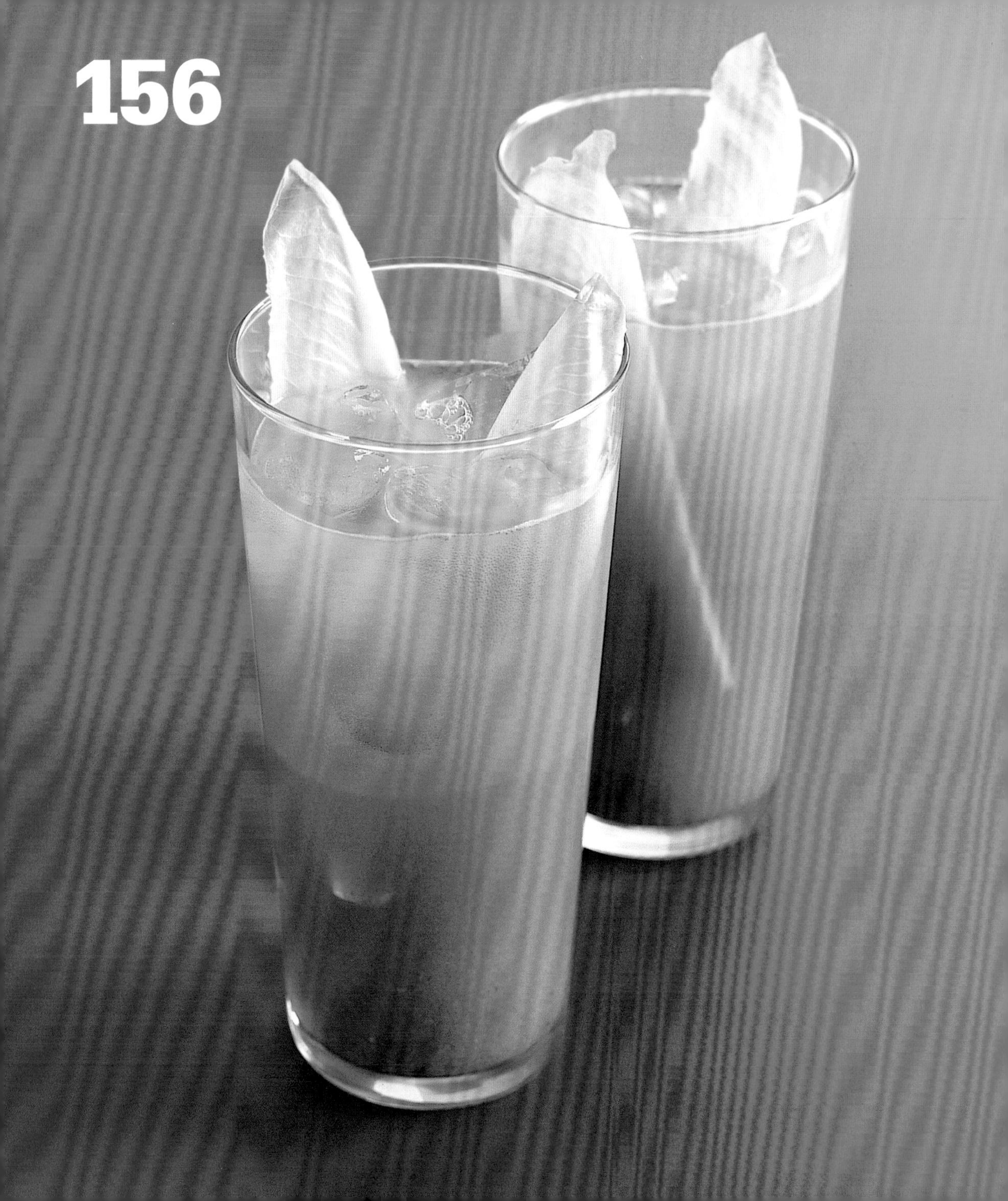

NUTRITIONAL CONTENT: energy 137 kcals | calcium 73 mg | magnesium 34 mg | zinc 0.4 mg | vitamin C 25 mg | vitamin A 41 mcg.

125 g (4 oz) pineapple

125 g (4 oz) grapes

50 g (2 oz) lettuce

50 g (2 oz) celery

chicory (endive) leaves, to decorate

ice cubes

Pineapple and grapes give a boost of blood sugar, which can help to induce sleep. Lettuce and celery relax the nerves and muscles.

1 Juice all the ingredients together and serve in a tall glass over ice. Decorate with chicory leaves.

makes 200 ml (7 fl oz)

sleep tight

morning after

125 g (4 oz) papaya, plus slices, to decorate

2 oranges

125 g (4 oz) cucumber, plus slices, to decorate

ice cubes

Papaya helps to calm the digestive system, cucumber flushes out toxins and orange gives a great boost of vitamin C. The overall effect is calming and rehydrating.

1 Peel the papaya and the oranges, leaving as much pith on the oranges as possible. Juice them together with the cucumber and serve in a tall glass over ice. Decorate with the extra slices of cucumber and papaya.

makes 200 ml (7 fl oz)

NUTRITIONAL CONTENT: energy 187 kcals I **calcium** 203 mg I **magnesium** 52 mg I **zinc** 0.9 mg I **vitamin C** 267 mg I **vitamin A** 175 mcg.

159

herbi-four

175 g (6 oz) red pepper

175 g (6 oz) tomatoes

100 g (3½ oz) white cabbage

1 tablespoon chopped parsley

lime wedges, to decorate

ice cubes

This juice is particularly good for the skin, which as the body's largest organ of elimination is the barometer of health and therefore the first to show any imbalances.

1 Juice the red pepper, tomatoes and cabbage. Pour into a tall glass over ice, stir in the parsley, decorate with thin wedges of lime and serve with a straw.

makes 200 ml (7 fl oz)

NUTRITIONAL CONTENT: energy 114 kcals | **calcium** 85 mg | **magnesium** 44 mg | **zinc** 0.6 mg | **vitamin C** 319 mg | **vitamin A** 1347 mcg.

vision impeccable

175 g (6 oz) carrot

125 g (4 oz) chicory (endive)

125 g (4 oz) celery

to serve

lemon slices

1 teaspoon chopped parsley

Carrots contain high levels of betacarotene and vitamin E, which are necessary for maintaining healthy eyes. Chicory is helpful in preventing cataracts. This combination of vegetables provides vitamin A to nourish the optic nerve.

1 Juice the carrot, chicory and celery. Whizz in a blender with a couple of ice cubes and serve with lemon slices and chopped parsley stirred in.

makes 200 ml (7 fl oz)

NUTRITIONAL CONTENT: energy 78 kcals I **calcium** 166 mg I **magnesium** 35 mg I **zinc** 0.7 mg I **vitamin C** 32 mg I **vitamin A** 1656 mcg.

200 ml (7 fl oz) soya milk

2 kiwi fruits, peeled

100 g (3½ oz) strawberries, hulled

25 g (1 oz) flaked almonds, to decorate

ice cubes

A delicious drink, rich in vitamins C and E and fibre. It is also a good source of calcium, and the soya milk is both calming and sleep-inducing.

1 Put all the ingredients in a food processor or blender. Add a few ice cubes, then process until smooth. Pour into a glass and decorate with flaked almonds.

makes 300 ml (½ pint)

sleeping beauty

feelin' good

75 g (3 oz) blueberries

1 teaspoon honey

25 g (1 oz) creamed coconut

100 ml (3½ fl oz) boiling water

1 small banana

2 tablespoons lime juice

4 tablespoons natural yogurt

This creamy concoction has a feel-good factor, but is still amazingly nutritious. Banana provides energy, fibre and minerals and blueberries are rich in vitamin C.

1 Blend the blueberries with half the honey to a purée and pour into sections of an ice cube tray. Freeze for at least 1 hour.

2 Chop the coconut into pieces and mix with the boiling water until the coconut has dissolved. Leave to cool.

3 Put the banana, lime juice, yogurt, coconut mixture and remaining honey in a blender and blend until completely smooth, scraping the mixture down from the sides of the bowl if necessary.

4 Place the blueberry ice cubes into a tall glass and add the smoothie. Stir lightly so the ice starts to melt.

makes 300 ml (½ pint)

NUTRITIONAL CONTENT: energy 427 kcals I **calcium** 336 mg I **magnesium** 85 mg I **zinc** 1.8 mg I **vitamin C** 47 mg I **vitamin A** 25 mcg.

beauty fuel

1 orange

100 g (3½ oz) sugarsnap peas, plus extra, sliced, to decorate

½ avocado

2–3 teaspoons lemon juice

mineral water

generous grating of nutmeg

Tired skin will benefit from a regular dose of this avocado smoothie. The sugarsnaps and orange juice add tangy goodness and nutmeg has calming, soothing properties. A good stop-gap between meals.

1 Cut away the skin from the orange and roughly chop the flesh. Push through the juicer with the sugarsnap peas. Pour the juice into a blender with the avocado and blend until smooth.

2 Stir in a little lemon juice to taste and add a dash of mineral water if the mixture is too thick. Pour into a glass and add plenty of freshly grated nutmeg and top with finely sliced sugarsnaps.

makes 200 ml (7 fl oz)

NUTRITIONAL CONTENT: energy 189 kcals | **calcium** 139 mg | **magnesium** 58 mg | **zinc** 1 mg | **vitamin C** 127 mg | **vitamin A** 42 mcg.

smooth operator

250 g (8 oz) carrot

100 g (3½ oz) figs, plus wedges to serve

1 orange

2.5 cm (1 inch) cube of fresh root ginger

100 g (3½ oz) banana

ice cubes

Bananas and figs are rich in tryptophan, necessary for the production of serotonin, which induces a feeling of well-being – great for fighting the winter blues.

1 Juice the carrot, figs, orange and ginger. Put the juice into a blender with the banana and 2 ice cubes and whizz for 20 seconds for a delicious smoothie. Layer more ice cubes and the fig wedges in a glass, pour the smoothie over them and serve with a stirrer.

makes 200 ml (7 fl oz)

NUTRITIONAL CONTENT: energy 262 kcals I **calcium** 187 mg I **magnesium** 84 mg I **zinc** 1.1 mg I **vitamin C** 88 mg I **vitamin A** 2256 mcg.

NUTRITIONAL CONTENT: **energy** 75 kcals | **calcium** 51 mg | **magnesium** 16 mg | **zinc** 0.2 mg | **vitamin C** 115 mg | **vitamin A** 2107 mcg.

2 carrots

15 g (½ oz) fresh root ginger

1 red pepper, deseeded

1 leafy celery stick

ice cubes

Carrots are good for the eyesight as they are rich in vitamin E and betacarotene. Here they are combined with red peppers and ginger, which help to keep infection at bay, and celery, which has an instantly soothing effect. This makes a good all-round supercooler.

1 Push the carrots and ginger, then the pepper, through a juicer. Pour into a glass and serve with the celery stick and several ice cubes.

makes 150 ml (¼ pint)

seeing red

peach dream

1 large juicy peach

4 ready-to-eat dried apricots

juice of 1 large orange

1 teaspoon mild honey

2 tablespoons mineral water

4 tablespoons Greek yogurt

fizzy water (optional) and ice cubes

Smooth and creamy, this is a drink to linger over after a hectic day. Peaches are rich in betacarotene which converts to vitamin A, a great nutrient for the skin, complexion and the immune system.

1 Stone and roughly chop the peach and put in a blender with the apricots and orange juice. Blend until smooth, scraping the mixture down from the sides of the bowl if necessary.

2 Stir in the honey and mineral water to thin the consistency slightly. Using a teaspoon, dot the yogurt all around the sides of a tall glass. Pour the peach juice into the glass and swirl the yogurt into the juice with the teaspoon. Top up with fizzy water, if liked, and serve with ice cubes.

makes 200 ml (7 fl oz)

NUTRITIONAL CONTENT: energy 470 kcals I **calcium** 366 mg I **magnesium** 90 mg I **zinc** 1.6 mg I **vitamin C** 96 mg I **vitamin A** 326 mcg.

175

bean good

50 g (2 oz) broccoli

1 apple

1 pear

75 g (3 oz) beansprouts

ice cubes

The combination of calcium, minerals and vitamins contained in broccoli makes this a great tonic for hair, teeth and bones. Combined with apples, pears and beansprouts, this is a blend to put you in mint condition. Use the ingredients straight from the refrigerator so they are refreshingly cold.

1 Cut the broccoli, apple and pear into pieces and push through the juicer with the beansprouts. Pour into a glass and serve over ice immediately.

makes 200 ml (7 fl oz)

NUTRITIONAL CONTENT: energy 147 kcals I **calcium** 64 mg I **magnesium** 40 mg I **zinc** 0.8 mg I **vitamin C** 64 mg I **vitamin A** 60 mcg.

177

rosy glow

½ **red-skinned apple**

3 **rosemary sprigs, plus extra, to serve**

½ **teaspoon herb honey**

200 **ml (7 fl oz) boiling water**

squeeze of lemon juice

Rosemary stimulates the circulation and soothes aching joints by increasing blood supply. It's also very good for promoting healthy hair. Rosemary is delicious with almost any fruit and this apple tea is particularly soothing. To reap all the benefits, eat the apple slices afterwards.

1 Core the apple and cut into thick slices. Put in a cup or teapot with the rosemary and honey and add the boiling water. Leave to infuse for 4–5 minutes and add the lemon juice before serving.

makes 200 ml (7 fl oz)

NUTRITIONAL CONTENT: energy 37 kcals I **calcium** 10 mg I **magnesium** 4 mg I **zinc** 0.1 mg I **vitamin C** 5 mg I **vitamin A** 3 mcg.

179

soothing brew

**3 chamomile flowerheads or
1 chamomile tea bag**

**1 lemon verbena flower spray,
plus 2 leaves**

½ teaspoon mild honey

200 ml (7 fl oz) boiling water

lemon slice, to serve

Chamomile tea is most frequently drunk as a late-night soother, but also aids digestion and treats anxiety and nerves. Here it is combined with lemon verbena, which also has calming properties.

1 Put the chamomile and verbena in a cup with the honey and add the boiling water. Leave to infuse for 4–5 minutes, no longer or the tea might become bitter. Serve with a slice of lemon.

makes 200 ml (7 fl oz)

NUTRITIONAL CONTENT: energy 14 kcals I **calcium** 4 mg I **magnesium** 2 mg I **zinc** 0 mg I **vitamin C** 0 mg I **vitamin A** 0 mcg.

3 sprigs lavender

½ teaspoon mild honey

200 ml (7 fl oz) boiling water

Lavender tea relaxes the mind and body and helps to achieve a good night's sleep. The flavour is an acquired taste, so add a squeeze of lemon juice or infuse some pared orange rind with the flowers if you like.

1 Put the lavender sprigs in a cup with their stalk ends uppermost so they can easily be lifted out. Add the honey and boiling water and leave to infuse for 4–5 minutes before serving.

makes 200 ml (7 fl oz)

pillow talk

eat your greens

1 Savoy cabbage

2 large onions

4 garlic cloves

875 g (1¾ lb) canned chopped tomatoes

2 green peppers

2 celery sticks

6 carrots

250 g (8 oz) green beans, sliced

2–3 tablespoons vegetable bouillon powder

oregano and thyme

600 ml (1 pint) vegetable stock

pepper

Cabbage soup is a healthy and effective way to help you lose weight, as well as making a nutritious detoxifying soup that is excellent for cleansing the colon and ridding the body of toxins. Be aware that this diet approach should only be undertaken under medical supervision, and is certainly no substitute for a healthy balanced diet. Try varying the texture and the seasonings to keep the inevitable feelings of monotony at bay.

1 Put all the ingredients into a large pan. Bring to the boil and reduce to a simmer until the vegetables are soft. Add a little water if the soup looks too thick. Season to taste with pepper and serve hot or cold.

makes 10 small portions

NUTRITIONAL CONTENT: energy 80 kcals | **protein** 4 g | **fat** 1 g | **carbohydrate** 15 g | **calcium** 86 mg | **iron** 1.9 mg | **vitamin C** 85 mg.

summer soup

750 g (1½ lb) ripe nectarines, peeled and stoned

250 ml (8 fl oz) freshly squeezed grapefruit juice

125 ml (4 fl oz) white grape juice or dry white wine

¼ teaspoon Tabasco sauce

1 tablespoon balsamic vinegar

2 tablespoons chopped fresh coriander

salt and pepper

Nectarines are low in calories yet one large nectarine provides almost three-quarters of the daily vitamin C requirement. The fruit has a gentle laxative effect and is also rich in iron and potassium.

1 Purée the nectarines in a food processor with the grapefruit juice, grape juice or wine, Tabasco sauce and balsamic vinegar. Add salt and pepper to taste.

2 Chop the coriander roughly and add to the nectarine mix, then cover and chill. Serve the soup in small bowls or cups.

makes 4 portions

NUTRITIONAL CONTENT: energy 111 kcals I **protein** 3 g I **fat** 1 g I **carbohydrate** 26 g I **calcium** 31 mg I **iron** 1.2 mg I **vitamin C** 90 mg.

188

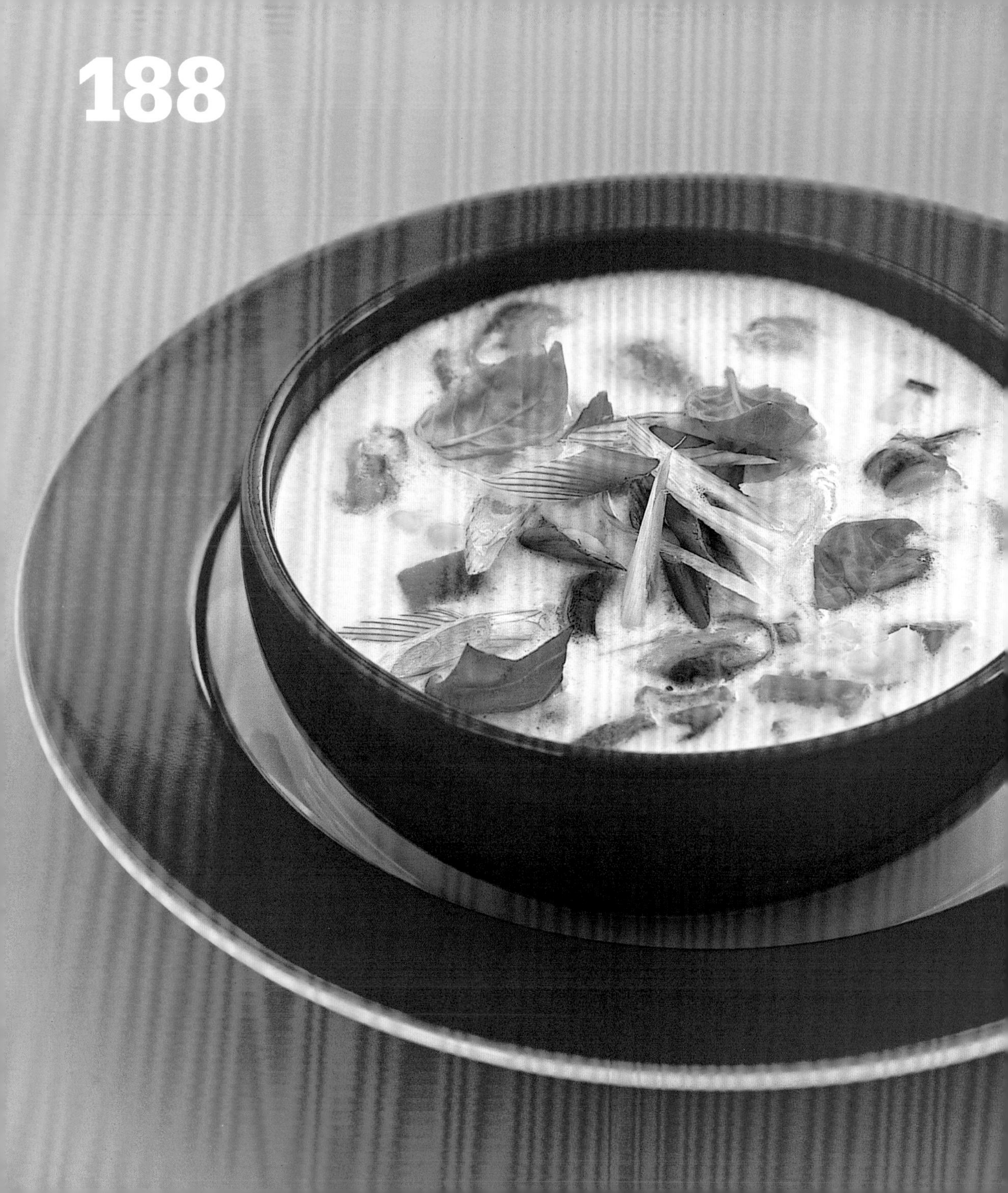

NUTRITIONAL CONTENT: energy 158 kcals | protein 15 g | fat 3 g | carbohydrate 16 g | calcium 212 mg | iron 6.8 mg | vitamin C 18 mg.

1½ kg (3 lb) mussels

150 ml (¼ pint) dry white wine

4 shallots, finely chopped

1 litre (1¾ pints) canned coconut milk

½ tablespoon finely chopped fresh root ginger

3 plum tomatoes, skinned, deseeded and roughly chopped

2 large chillies, deseeded and chopped

4 tablespoons canned sweetcorn kernels

to garnish

1 spring onion, finely sliced

2 tablespoons basil leaves

Seafood is universally hailed as brain food and, as it is high in zinc, it is a beneficial addition to the diet when stress levels are high. Zinc helps to break down alcohol and is a vital component of insulin, which controls blood sugar levels.

1 Wash the mussels in cold water. Pull off their beards and discard any mussels that are open and do not close when tapped on a hard surface.

2 Put the wine and shallots into a large saucepan and boil for about 2–3 minutes. Add the mussels and boil for 2 minutes, or until all the mussels have opened. Immediately drain them over a bowl. As soon as they are cool enough to handle, carefully pull them from their shells, discarding any that have not opened. Reserve the broth and the mussels.

3 Strain the mussel broth into a large pan, discarding any grit or dirt that may have sunk to the bottom. Add the coconut milk, ginger, tomatoes, chillies and sweetcorn. Heat and simmer for 2 minutes, then add the mussels.

4 Serve the soup in warmed bowls sprinkled with spring onion and basil leaves.

makes 6 portions

mussel power

juicy lucy

200 g (7 oz) watermelon

200 g (7 oz) strawberries, plus extra, to decorate

1 mint sprig, to decorate

Watermelon is the ideal detoxifier, the flesh is packed with betacarotene and vitamin C. By adding strawberries, you'll be receiving a great boost of vitamin C as well as helping fight bacteria in your system. Rich in zinc and potassium, two great eliminators.

1 Juice the fruit and whizz in a blender with a couple of ice cubes. Serve decorated with a sprig of mint and the extra strawberries.

makes 200 ml (7 fl oz)

NUTRITIONAL CONTENT: energy 116 kcals I **calcium** 46 mg I **magnesium** 36 mg I **zinc** 0.6 mg I **vitamin C** 170 mg I **vitamin A** 79 mcg.

flush-a-bye-baby

250 g (8 oz) cranberries

250 g (8 oz) watermelon or Galia melon, plus sticks, to serve

250 g (8 oz) cucumber

The cucumber in this juice provides protective antioxidants for the digestive tract and, combined with the melon, acts as a diuretic to cleanse the intestinal system. Good for cystitis.

1 Juice all the ingredients together, including the pips of the melon and the skin of the cucumber. Serve in a tumbler and decorate with a couple of melon sticks.

makes 200 ml (7 fl oz)

NUTRITIONAL CONTENT: energy 140 kcals I **calcium** 93 mg I **magnesium** 58 mg I **zinc** 1.3 mg I **vitamin C** 58 mg I **vitamin A** 131 mcg.

193

NUTRITIONAL CONTENT: energy 142 kcals | calcium 156 mg | magnesium 34 mg | zinc 0.9 mg | vitamin C 96 mg | vitamin A 197 mcg.

250 g (8 oz) pear

125 g (4 oz) cabbage

50 g (2 oz) celery, plus a stick, to decorate

25 g (1 oz) watercress

ice cubes

Cabbage is a great detoxifier. It aids digestion and prevents fluid retention and constipation. Watercress is a powerful intestinal cleanser, the cabbage and the pear rid the colon of waste matter and the celery purifies the lymph.

1 Juice all the ingredients together and serve in a glass over ice, decorated with a celery stick.

makes 200 ml (7 fl oz)

spring clean

squeaky green

175 g (6 oz) carrot

75 g (3 oz) celery

100 g (3½ oz) spinach

100 g (3½ oz) lettuce

25 g (1 oz) parsley, plus extra to decorate

ice cubes

This juice will prevent the build-up of toxins in your system which leads to sluggish metabolism, low energy and possibly serious illnesses. Carrots, lettuce, spinach and celery all work to regenerate the liver and lymph system and aid digestion. Parsley is good for kidney stones.

1 Juice the ingredients and whizz in a blender with a couple of ice cubes. Decorate with sprigs of parsley.

makes 200 ml (7 fl oz)

NUTRITIONAL CONTENT: energy 106 kcals I **calcium** 344 mg I **magnesium** 86 mg I **zinc** 1.5 mg I **vitamin C** 93 mg I **vitamin A** 2379 mcg.

197

orchard medley

75 g (3 oz) ready-to-eat stoned prunes

100 g (3½ oz) blackberries

100 ml (3½ fl oz) apple juice

1 teaspoon clear honey

1 apple wedge, to decorate

You can make this detoxifying smoothie at any time of year as frozen blackberries make a good substitute for fresh. Juice your own Bramley apples or use a good quality tart apple juice to counteract the sweetness of the prunes.

1 Put the prunes and blackberries in a blender and blend until smooth, scraping the mixture down from the sides of the bowl if necessary.

2 Add the apple juice and blend until completely smooth. Taste and add a little honey if the mixture is too sharp. Serve in a tall glass, decorated with an apple wedge.

makes 250 ml (8 fl oz)

NUTRITIONAL CONTENT: energy 192 kcals I **calcium** 74 mg I **magnesium** 46 mg I **zinc** 0.6 mg I **vitamin C** 29 mg I **vitamin A** 31 mcg.

199

tropical trio

½ small mango, peeled, plus a wedge, to decorate

1 thick slice of pineapple, peeled

½ small papaya

juice of ½ orange

squeeze of lime juice

Mango, papaya and pineapple are packed with betacarotene and vitamin C and make a delicious detox blend. This quantity makes one long drink but you can make a larger batch for a chilled supply.

1 Roughly chop the mango and pineapple and put in a blender. Discard the seeds from the papaya and scoop the flesh into the blender.

2 Add the orange and lime juice and blend until completely smooth, scraping the mixture down from the sides of the bowl if necessary. Serve in a tall glass, decorated with a wedge of mango.

makes 300 ml (½ pint)

NUTRITIONAL CONTENT: energy 138 kcals I **calcium** 57 mg I **magnesium** 37 mg I **zinc** 0.6 mg I **vitamin C** 147 mg I **vitamin A** 326 mcg.

strawberry cleanser

125 g cranberries or 100 ml (3½ fl oz) unsweetened cranberry juice

125 g (4 oz) strawberries

100 g (3½ oz) seedless red or black grapes

Cranberries are renowned for their cleansing properties and like all red fruits are packed with vitamin C and cancer-fighting chemicals. For best results make this smoothie when strawberries are at their sweetest and juiciest, otherwise you might need to add a little honey to sweeten.

1 If using whole cranberries, push them through a juicer. Pour the juice into a blender or food processor.

2 Hull the strawberries and put in the blender with the grapes. Blend until smooth, scraping the mixture down from the sides of the bowl if necessary. Serve immediately.

makes 300 ml (½ pint)

NUTRITIONAL CONTENT: energy 143 kcals | **calcium** 33 mg | **magnesium** 20 mg | **zinc** 0.2 mg | **vitamin C** 129 mg | **vitamin A** 5 mcg.

203

lemon barley water

rind of 1 unwaxed lemon, cut into fine strips, plus extra to decorate

2 tablespoons barley

1.2 litres (2 pints) boiling water

sugar, to taste

ice cubes

What could be more soothing and relaxing than the fresh taste of home-made lemon barley water – a perfect summer detox drink at the end of a tiring day.

1 Put the lemon rind into a heatproof jug with the barley. Pour over the boiling water and stir well. Cover and leave to stand overnight.

2 Add sugar to taste, then strain the barley water through a piece of muslin – it should be clear.

3 To serve, fill glasses with ice cubes, pour in the lemon barley water and decorate with fine strips of lemon rind.

makes 900 ml (1½ pints)

NUTRITIONAL CONTENT: energy 85 kcals I **calcium** 6 mg I **magnesium** 7 mg I **zinc** 0.2 mg I **vitamin C** 3 mg I **vitamin A** 0 mcg.

205

red devil

125 g (4 oz) beetroot

1 carrot

½ mild red chilli

1 orange

crushed ice

Beetroot is a good blood-builder and an excellent cleanser for the intestine and liver. It's also rich in calcium, vitamin C and minerals. Oranges and carrots are also vital ingredients for a detox diet, so keep a fresh supply.

1 Roughly chop the beetroot, carrot and chilli. Cut away the skin from the orange and roughly chop the flesh. Push the beetroot, carrot and chilli, then the orange, through a juicer. Serve with crushed ice.

makes 200 ml (7 fl oz)

NUTRITIONAL CONTENT: energy 132 kcals I **calcium** 120 mg I **magnesium** 33 mg I **zinc** 0.7 mg I **vitamin C** 102 mg I **vitamin A** 889 mcg.

NUTRITIONAL CONTENT: energy 113 kcals | calcium 54 mg | magnesium 17 mg | zinc 0.3 mg | vitamin C 16 mg | vitamin A 13 mcg.

2 celery sticks

1 crisp apple

100 g (3½ oz) green grapes

ice cubes

This drink contains three very effective cleansers in one long cooler, and it's easy enough on the tastebuds to drink on a regular basis. All the ingredients provide vitamin C.

1 Chop the celery sticks and apple and push through the juicer with the grapes. Serve with plenty of ice cubes.

makes 300 ml (½ pint)

freshen up

herbal harmony

3–4 parsley sprigs

3–4 mint sprigs

15 g (½ oz) fresh root ginger, peeled

200 ml (7 fl oz) boiling water

1 teaspoon herb honey

This combination may sound unusual but it will give you a thoroughly good cleanse. Parsley is rich in vitamins and iron and is a diuretic herb, used in the treatment of fluid retention. Ginger and mint are both good for digestion and give the infusion a lift.

1 Put the parsley and mint sprigs, including the stalks, in a cup. Thinly slice the ginger and add to the cup with the boiling water.

2 Leave to infuse for 4–5 minutes then lift out the herbs and ginger, if liked. Stir in a little honey to taste.

makes 200 ml (7 fl oz)

NUTRITIONAL CONTENT: energy 33 kcals I **calcium** 20 mg I **magnesium** 1 mg I **zinc** 0.1 mg I **vitamin C** 9 mg I **vitamin A** 33 mcg.

digestive duo

½ fennel bulb, plus stalks, to decorate

1 juicy pear

100 ml (3½ fl oz) boiling water

Fennel and pear work well together, not only in flavour but because they're both effective diuretics and digestive aids. Pears also contain pectin which helps flush out toxins from the body.

1 Roughly chop the fennel and pear into pieces and push through the juicer. Pour the juice into a small pan and add the boiling water. Heat gently until hot but not boiling and pour into a cup.

makes 200 ml (7 fl oz)

NUTRITIONAL CONTENT: energy 72 kcals | **calcium** 41 mg | **magnesium** 19 mg | **zinc** 0.7 mg | **vitamin C** 14 mg | **vitamin A** 28 mcg.

dynamic detox

8 dandelion leaves, torn into pieces

200 ml (7 fl oz) boiling water

1 tablespoon lemon juice

2 teaspoons clear honey

Dandelion leaves are one of the most effective detox foods, powerfully diuretic but rich in the essential minerals that might be lost during a detox regime. Lemon, like all citrus fruits, is a good cleanser and packed with vital vitamins.

1 Put the dandelion leaves in a cup and pour over the boiling water. Leave to infuse for 4 minutes then lift out the leaves. Stir in the lemon juice and honey and serve.

makes 200 ml (7 fl oz)

NUTRITIONAL CONTENT: energy 53 kcals | **calcium** 24 mg | **magnesium** 8 mg | **zinc** 0.2 mg | **vitamin C** 5 mg | **vitamin A** 7 mcg.

minty magic

1 large Spanish onion, chopped

2 garlic cloves, roughly chopped

250 g (8 oz) leek, roughly chopped

1.5 litres (2½ pints) chicken or vegetable stock

250 g (8 oz) canned butter beans

1 thyme sprig

1 bay leaf

250 g (8 oz) mangetout

1 bunch of mint, leaves removed from the stalks

salt and pepper

to garnish

1 tablespoon fromage frais

2 tablespoons caviar or fish roe, black or red

Peas and beans are very high in fibre and detoxify the digestive system. The onion, leek and garlic will help purify the blood and vital organs.

1 Sweat the onion, garlic and leek with a little stock, covered, in a large saucepan until softened. Add the butter beans, remaining stock and the thyme and bay leaf and boil for 10 minutes, then reduce the heat and simmer gently for 20 minutes.

2 Add the mangetout and the mint leaves, reserving a few leaves for garnish, and boil for 5 minutes. Transfer to a food processor and blend until smooth.

3 Pass the soup through a fine sieve, return to the pan and season with salt and pepper to taste. Serve the soup in warmed bowls, with a swirl of fromage frais and a dollop of caviar or fish roe. Finish each bowl with a mint leaf and serve immediately.

makes 4 portions

NUTRITIONAL CONTENT: energy 176 kcals I **protein** 12 g I **fat** 3 g I **carbohydrate** 27 g I calcium 104 mg I iron 4 mg I **vitamin C** 48 mg.

217

NUTRITIONAL CONTENT: energy 70 kcals | protein 2 g | fat 4 g | carbohydrate 8 g | calcium 34 mg | iron 1.3 mg | vitamin C 37 mg.

750 g (1½ lb) ripe red tomatoes

1 large fennel bulb

300 ml (½ pint) boiling water

1 teaspoon rock salt

¾ teaspoon coriander seeds

½ teaspoon mixed peppercorns

1 tablespoon extra virgin olive oil

1 large garlic clove, crushed

1 small onion, chopped

1 tablespoon balsamic vinegar

1 tablespoon lemon juice

¾ teaspoon chopped oregano

1 teaspoon tomato purée

This light, vitamin-packed soup is ideal for a summer detox and perfect for boosting the immune system. Fennel is a natural diuretic and is also rich in phytoestrogens. It is good for calming hot flushes.

1 Pour boiling water over the tomatoes and leave for about 1 minute. Drain and remove the skins, then chop roughly.

2 Trim the green fronds from the fennel and reserve. Thinly slice the bulb and put it into a saucepan with the boiling water and the rock salt. Cover and simmer for 10 minutes.

3 Crush the coriander seeds and peppercorns using a pestle and mortar. Heat the olive oil in a large saucepan and add the crushed spices, garlic and onion. Cook gently for 5 minutes.

4 Add the balsamic vinegar, lemon juice, tomatoes and oregano and stir well. Add the fennel with its cooking liquid and the tomato purée. Bring to a simmer and leave to cook uncovered for 30 minutes.

5 Blend the soup to a purée in a food processor. Let it cool then chill for at least 2 hours. Serve the soup garnished with the reserved fennel fronds.

makes 4 portions

feel-good fennel

orient express

1 litre (1¾ pints) water

75 g (3 oz) dashi granules

100 g (3½ oz) miso

1 tablespoon mirin or
dry sherry

250 g (8 oz) firm tofu, cut
into cubes

to garnish

1 spring onion, diagonally
sliced

1 sheet of toasted nori seaweed,
crumbled into small pieces

Miso is a soya bean paste; it contains powerful isoflavones and is thought to protect against breast and prostate cancer. Soya-rich foods are also believed to reduce LDL (bad cholesterol). Dashi is a Japanese fish-based stock.

1 Using a wooden spoon, combine the water and dashi granules in a small saucepan, then bring the mixture to the boil. Reduce the heat to medium, add the miso and mirin and stir to combine, taking care the mixture does not boil as overheating will result in a loss of flavour.

2 Add the tofu cubes to the hot stock and heat without boiling over a medium heat for 5 minutes. Serve in warm bowls sprinkled with the spring onion and nori.

makes 4 portions

NUTRITIONAL CONTENT: energy 108 kcals I **protein** 10 g I **fat** 4 g I **carbohydrate** 6 g I **calcium** 360 mg I **iron** 2.8 mg I **vitamin C** 1 mg.

index

acher shaker 96, *97*
ailment chart 10–11
alfalfa sprouts 127
almonds 6, 112
apple juice 133, 198
apples 6, 52, 64, 82, 92, 120, 122, 127, 130, 136, 146, 176, 178, 206
apricot juice 134
apricots 6, 94, 134, 174
asparagus 6, 111
avocados 6, 94, 130, 168

bananas 6, 56, 58, 61, 92, 96, 128, 166, 170
barley 6, 204
basil 40
bay leaves 44
bean good 176, *177*
beans, green 184
beansprouts 176
beauty fuel 168, *169*
beet this *102*, 103
beetroot 6, 18, 49, 54, 103, 122, 208
belly berry 82, *83*
berried treasure 148, *149*
berry mull 72, *73*
berry nice 128, *129*
bionic tonic 56, *57*
black bean bonanza 78, 79
black-eyed beans 78

black pepper 6
blackberries 6, 20, 136, 198
blackcurrants 108
blood orange 62, *63*
blueberries 6, 72, 82, 120, 128, 166
brain booster 152, *153*
broccoli 6, 18, 151, 176
bumpy ride 122, *123*
butter beans 216

c for comfort 108, *109*
cabbages 6, 160, 184, 195
cantaloupe melons 16, 20, 28, 68
cardamom 16, 104, 114
caribbean spice 76, 77
carrot juice 28
carrots 7, 16, 18, 44, 49, 50, 78, 80, 88, 116, 124, 142, 151, 162, 170, 173, 184, 196, 208
carroty cooler 28, *29*
celery 7, 78, 80, 111, 122, 130, 142, 151, 154, 157, 162, 184, 195, 196, 206
chamomile 181
chicken 111
chicory (endive) 162
chill-out 112, *113*
chillies 114, 152, 189, 208

chunky chowder *150*, 151
cinnamon 7, 70, 146
citrus squeeze 140, *141*
classic c & c 44, *45*
cleansing cranberry 146, *147*
clementines 36
cloves 114, 148
coconut 7, 77, 90, 134, 152, 166, 189
cool and cleansing 136, *137*
coolers 4, 28–33, 62–7, 98–103, 136–42, 173–6, 204–8
coriander 7, 44, 114, 152, 186, 219
cranberries 7, 58, 146, 190, 202
cranberry juice 128
cucumbers 7, 30, 40, 86, 94, 98, 158, 190
cumin 74, 104, 114

dandelion leaves 214
dashi 220
digestive duo 212, *213*
dynamic detox 214, *215*

eat your greens 184, *185*
energy bubble 52, *53*
energy fizz *66*, 67
evergreen 154, *155*

feel-good fennel *218*, 219
feelin' good 166, *167*
fennel 7, 103, 142, 154, 212, 219
fever fusion 106, *107*
feverfew 106
fiery indian broth 114, *115*
figs 170
flush-a-bye-baby 190, *191*
freshen up 206, *207*
frisky sour 12, *13*
fruity filler 134, *135*
full tank *126*, 127

Galia melons 94, 190
garlic 7, 40, 43, 44, 74, 77, 78, 112, 114, 151, 152, 184, 216, 219
ginger 7, 16, 67, 77, 80, 100, 114, 120, 142, 146, 152, 170, 173, 189, 210
ginger spice 142, *143*
ginger zinger 16, *17*
golden fizz *32*, 33
grapefruits 7, 12, 88, 98, 120, 140, 187
grapes 7, 54, 70, 92, 103, 116, 157, 202, 206
great gazpacho 40, *41*
green dream 130, *131*
green tea 38, 104

health 4–5
herbal harmony 210, *211*
herbi-four 160, *161*
hibiscus flowers 106
high kick *60*, 61
honeydew melons 94
horseradish 7, 80
hot stuff 80, *81*
hula kula 90, *91*

infusions 4, 34–8, 68–72,
 104–8, 144–8, 178–82,
 210–14
ingredients 4, 6–8

juicers 5
juices 4, 12–20, 49–54,
 80–8, 116–24, 154–62,
 190–6
juicy lucy 190, *191*

karma kooler *98*, 99
kiwi fruits 20, 61, 86, *119*,
 130, 165

lavender 183
leeks 111, 151, 216
lemon balm 70
lemon barley water 204,
 205
lemon thyme 38
lemon verbena 181
lemongrass 34, 152
lemons 7, 58, 99, 106,
 130, 204, 214
lentil power 74, *75*
lentils 74, 114
lettuce 154, 157, 196

limes 7, 13, 17, 28, 34, 77,
 100, 138
lounge lizard 86, *87*

mangetout 216
mango magic 26, *27*
mangoes 7, 25, 26, 52, 56,
 92, 138, 200
melons 7, 17, 20, 28, 68,
 94, 95, 192
milk 58
mineral water 33, 99,
 168, 174
mint 14, 104, 210, 216
minty magic 216, *217*
miso 220
morning after 158, *159*
mushrooms 7, 43
mussel power *188*, 189
mussels 189

nectarines 187
nettles 34

onions 7, 40, 43, 44, 74,
 77, 78, 111, 114, 151,
 184, 216, 219
orange juice 25, 28, 33, 46
oranges 8, 14, 49, 51, 63,
 92, 144, 158, 168, 170,
 174, 200, 206
orchard medley 198, *199*
organic produce 5
orient express 220, *221*

papaya flyer 124, *125*
papayas 8, 12, 33, 124,
 152, 158, 200

parsley 8, 38, 160, 196,
 210
parsnips 8, 67
passion fruit plus 34, *35*
passion fruits 34, 52,
 138, 144
passion thriller 94, *95*
peach dream 174, *175*
peaches 8, 119, 174
pears 8, 67, 85, 124, 1
 76, 195, 212
peas, sugarsnap 168
pecan nuts 133
pecan punch *132*, 133
peppers 8, 14, 40, 160,
 173, 184
pillow talk *182*, 183
pineapple juice 56
pineapple sage 38
pineapples 8, 90, 92, 96,
 127, 154, 157, 200
pistachio nuts 134
plum punch *118*, 119
plums 54, 119
protein pack 22, *23*
pomegranate seeds 86
pomegranates 116
pomeloes 141
potatoes 43, 151
power pack *48*, 49
prunes 85, 198
purple passion 120, *121*

quick hit *24*, 25

raisins 134
raspberries 8, 12, 72, 128,
 148

rda table 9
recovery *110*, 111
red devil 206, *207*
red wire 54, *55*
redcurrants 63
rose royce 64, *65*
rosehips 64
rosemary 178
rosy glow 178, *179*

seeing red *172*, 173
sergeant pepper 14, *15*
sesame seeds 58
simply strawberry 46, *47*
sleep tight *156*, 157
sleeping beauty *164,* 165
smooth and soothing 58,
 59
smooth operator 170, *171*
smoothies 4, 22–6, 56–61,
 90–6, 126–34, 164–70,
 198–202
soothing brew *180,* 181
soups 4, 40–6, 74–8,
 110–14, 151–2, 184–9,
 216–20
sour power 116, *117*
soya milk 8, 22, 90, 127,
 141, 151, 165
spinach 8, 85, 88, 114,
 196
spirulina 61, 142
spring clean 194, *195*
squash 151
squeaky green 196, *197*

223

star anise 68

star burst 68, *69*

stock 40, 43, 44, 74, 77, 78, 111, 112, 114, 151, 152, 184, 216

strawberries 8, 25, 46, 49, 61, 63, 72, 96, 165, 190, 202

strawberry cleanser 202, *203*

summer berries 22

summer soup 186, *187*

sweet chariot 92, *93*

sweet potatoes 8, 77

sweet stinger 34, *35*

sweetcorn 151, 189

tarragon 154

tchae trio 38, *39*

thyme 108

time out 20, *21*

tofu 8, 111, 152, 220

tomato juice 30

tomato tonic 30, *31*

tomatoes 8, 40, 80, 151, 160, 184, 189, 219

tongue tingler 144, *145*

tropical trio 200, *201*

tropicana 138, *139*

tummy tonic 104, *105*

twister 88, *89*

vanilla pods 72

vision impeccable 162, *163*

vitamin vitality *50,* 51

vitamins 9

warm and spicy 70, *71*

watercress 195

watermelons 190, 190

way to go *84,* 85

what's up broc? 18, *19*

wheat 8, 94

white grape juice 46

wild mushroom dream 42, 43

yogurt 8, 26, 56, 58, 114, 128, 133, 138, 166, 174

zesty ginger beer 100, *101*

acknowledgements

Executive editor: Sarah Ford

Project Editor: Kate Tuckett

Executive Art Editor: Geoff Fennell

Designer: Sue Michniewicz

Photographer: Stephen Conroy

Stylist: Angela Swaffield

Home Economists: Joanna Farrow, David Morgan

Production Controller: Aileen O'Reilly